Y0-AGU-358

FAMILY TRIVIA

AWE-INSPIRING FACTS & INTRIGUING ILLUSIONS

This edition published by Parragon Books Ltd in 2017

Parragon Books Ltd
Chartist House
15–17 Trim Street
Bath BA1 1HA, UK
www.parragon.com

ISBN 978-1-4748-6915-7

Printed in China

FAMILY TRIVIA

AWE-INSPIRING FACTS & INTRIGUING ILLUSIONS

300 AWESOME TRUTHS AND STARTLING VISUALS TO DAZE AND AMAZE!

INTRODUCTION

What we see in front of us cannot always be taken at face value and what we know about the world is constantly shifting and expanding. If you like to look below the surface, to explore what things really mean, to update your knowledge about the world and to observe things that don't quite seem possible, then this collection of *Awe-Inspiring Facts & Intriguing Illusions* will keep you on your toes. Every page will propel you from dazzling visual acrobatics, confounding shapes and bewildering sights to captivating facts, mind-boggling trivia and revelatory insights.

Did you know that the only English word starting and ending with a z is 'zizz'? Or that cats only need one eighth of the light of humans to be able to see? Or have you ever experienced geometric patterns that seem to buzz with invisible energy and draw you into their core? Or see colours in areas where, in fact, there are none?

Can you even tell straight from curved? Take a look at the red lines in the optical illusion on the next page – the red lines seem to bend, but they're really perfectly straight.

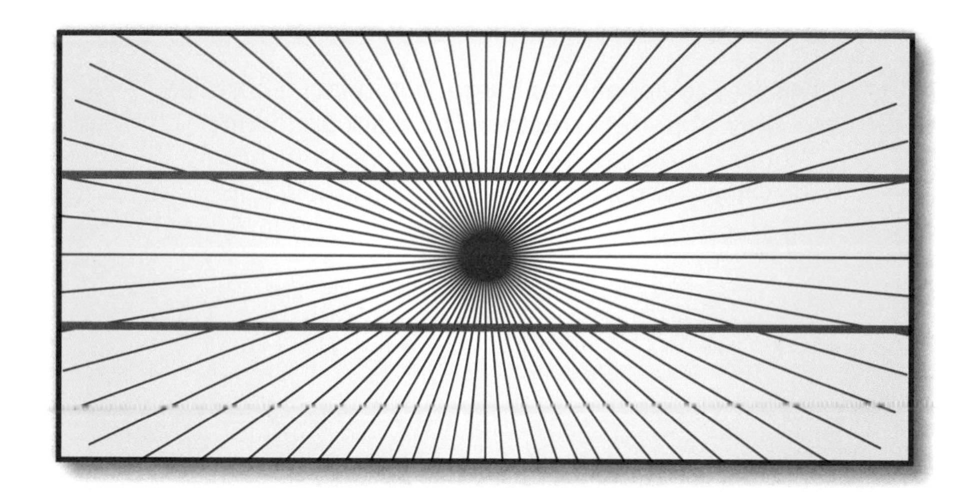

The facts and optical illusions are interspersed throughout the book, with each one simply identified by the icons below:

Fact

Optical illusion

So prepare to be amazed as you begin your journey into the world of magical and disorientating optical illusions and endlessly surprising and mind-boggling facts. Including startling visual tricks and fascinating facts about the invention of the tea bag, the nose design of a Proboscis monkey, the incredible strength of an egg and the number of different words for 'reindeer', you will come away both enlightened and stimulated.

SQUARE BULGE

This image appears to bulge, but in fact it consists only of perfect squares. The black and white intersecting squares are confusing your brain! Check with a ruler, if you need convincing.

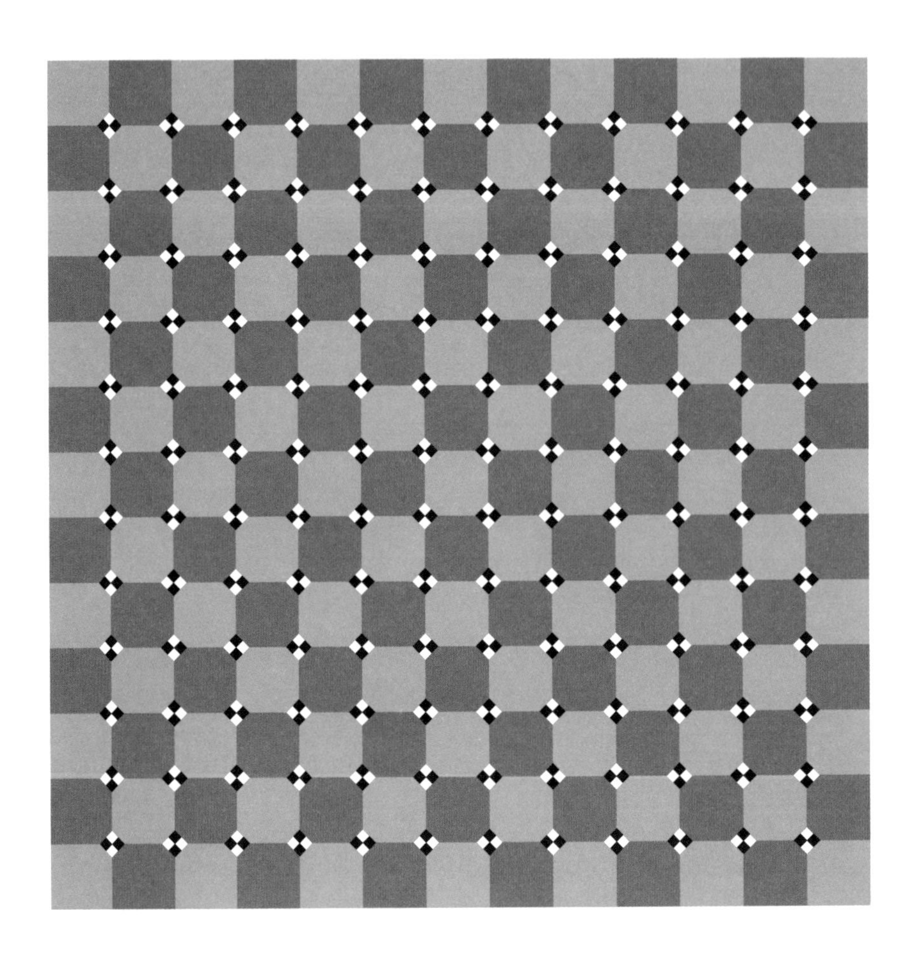

SHEEP OR GOAT?

In Chinese there is no specific word for 'goat' or 'sheep', so the eighth year of the twelve-year Chinese calendar cycle, yáng, is translated variously as either the Year of the Sheep or Ram, or as the Year of the Goat. It would more accurately be translated as the less catchy Year of the Caprinae, a subfamily which includes both sheep and goats.

LONG WORD

The longest word in any of Shakespeare's works is

honorificabilitudinitatibus

which consists of alternating consonants and vowels for its entire length! It means 'honourableness'.

REGULAR SHAPES?

At first glance this seems to be a regular nut, but you'd need a very strangely shaped bolt to screw this impossible shape onto!

Could you make this shape? It might look like a regular triangle, but trace your finger or eye around one of the edges and you'll soon spot something strange about it!

SUDOKU NUMBERS

		2						
		9	6	3	2			
		8				2	9	1
	9			1			3	
	3		2		4		5	
	5			6			4	
7	2	4				9		
			1	9	7	4		
						3		

If you've ever wondered just how few numbers are required to make a valid Sudoku puzzle, the answer is 17.
With fewer than that many given numbers, the puzzle does not have a unique solution. For a rotationally symmetrical puzzle, there must be at least 18 given numbers.

PROTECTIVE BLOUSES

In the 19th century blouses were worn by both men and women, only later becoming an item of clothing worn solely by women. The word derives from French. In that language, it means 'a protective garment'.

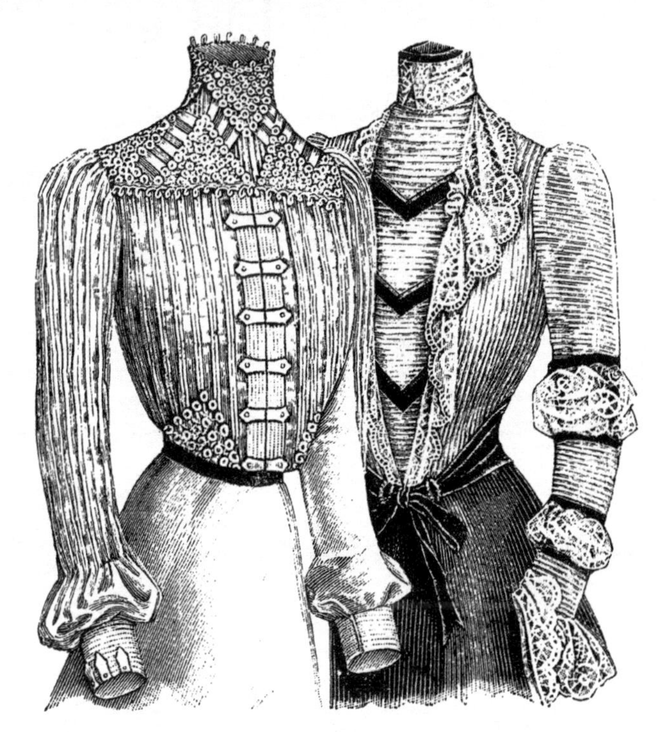

ACORN SHOOTS

Some types of oak tree, of which there are around 600 living species, do not start producing acorns until they are 20 years old, and some do not do so until they have been growing for 50 years! A mature oak will produce around 90,000 acorns each year.

CROC SIZE

Despite their name, saltwater crocodiles do not only live in salt water but are equally at home in fresh water. They can reach sizes of up to 7.1 m (23.3 ft) in length – that's about the height of two and a half storeys. Scarily, crocodiles can jump up out of water to a height equal to their length!

SHADES OF GREY

Look at the two grey tiles marked with dots. It's hard to believe, but they're both the same shade of grey!
Don't believe it? Make a small hole in a piece of paper and look at the tiles through it.

PULSE AND FLOW

Roll your eyes across this image. Freaky, isn't it? The blue shapes pulse and flow as your eyes pass by. This effect is caused by the contrasting white and black borders on each of the shapes.

HIGH JUMPER

The animal that can jump the furthest is thought to be the snow leopard, which has been observed leaping distances of 15 m (49 ft).

WHAT COLOUR?

Approximately 1 in 12 men, and around 1 in 200 women, have some form of colour blindness. The most common is red/green colour blindness, which means that they have trouble distinguishing between colours containing red and green light. Symptoms vary in severity, with about 40 per cent of those afflicted not realizing that they have the condition.

DON'T LOOK AWAY...

Stare into the centre of the book, and slowly move it closer and closer towards you.

The white area in the centre of the image slowly grows larger... and larger... and larger!

FISH MEMORY

There is a common myth that goldfish have a memory of only a few seconds, but this is false. In fact, experiments have proved that their memory is so good that they can be trained to perform tasks, such as pushing a lever to receive food, and can then remember this training for months afterwards.

DANCING BEES

Honeybees dance when they return to their hive to show the location of flowers, moving in figures of eight and waggling their behinds to indicate the precise location of interesting nectar, pollen and water sources – or even a new hive location.

DIAGONAL ACTION

These diagonal lines create a vivid, flashing interference pattern. The vertical divisions between each column also appear to bend slightly – although in reality this isn't true.

EVEN GREY

The central grey strip is exactly the same colour from top to bottom, yet it appears to change shade. The surrounding greys are influencing your perception.

LED TECH

Light-emitting diodes (LEDs) first appeared in 1962, but it was not until 1994 that the first practical blue LED was made, winning a Nobel prize for its three creators. Its invention paved the way for current ubiquitous screen and bulb technologies.

BRAIN ACTION

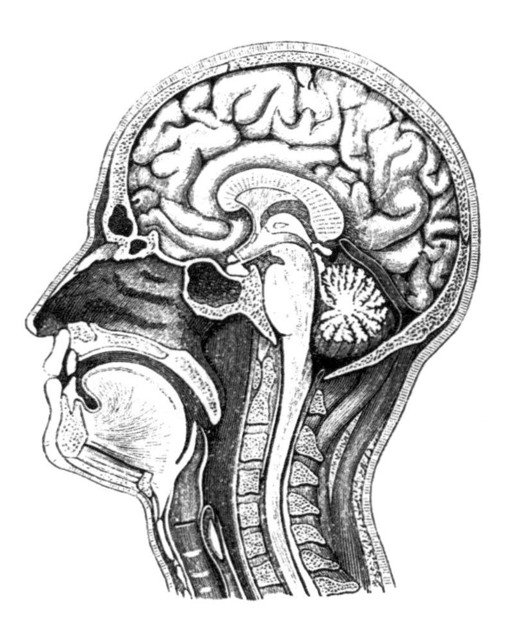

Each individual nerve cell in the brain can only hold a limited supply of energy, so the bloodstream is needed to supply extra energy to the cell to replenish it after use. This means that if you're not sufficiently fit and healthy that, quite literally, you will not be able to think as fast.

Your brain represents only 2 per cent of your body weight but uses 20 per cent of the body's energy.

FRESH WATER

Only 3 per cent of the water on Earth is fresh. The remaining 97 per cent is salt water.

DO AWAY WITH SOCKS

Albert Einstein was not a big fan of socks. Throughout his life he refused to wear them, even when attending a formal dinner at the White House. He felt that shoes were entirely sufficient and that socks simply created extra work.

HANGING ON

On initial inspection this might seem to be an ordinary picture of a vase on a shelf, with a mug hanging below.
But take a closer look and you'll see that all is not as it seems...

UPSIDE DOWN

It's a remarkable fact that if you were to wear spectacles that turned the entire world upside down, your brain could adapt to this new viewpoint within as little as three days. Experiments have also shown that the brain will rapidly adapt to many other visual distortions, such as angled views or views from outside the body.

BYTES AND NYBBLES

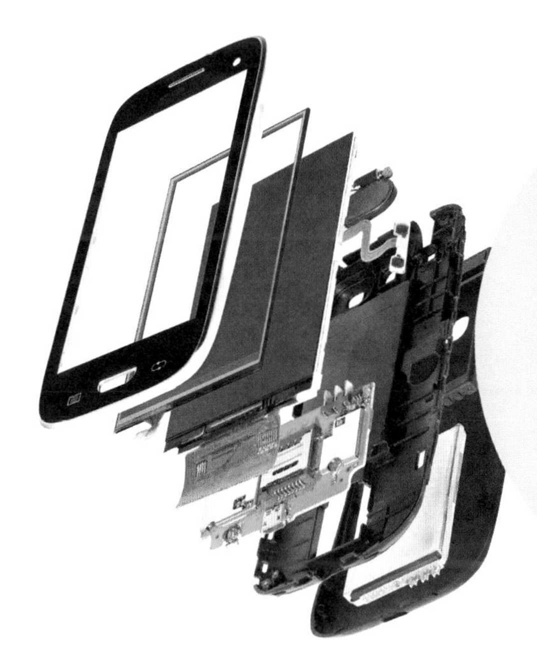

You might know how many megabytes or gigabytes your phone or computer has – and that's millions or billions of bytes, respectively. But did you know that half a byte is called a 'nybble'? And that a quarter of a 'nybble' is a 'bit'? A 'bit' is a single binary digit, either a '0' or a '1'.

SAME CIRCLES

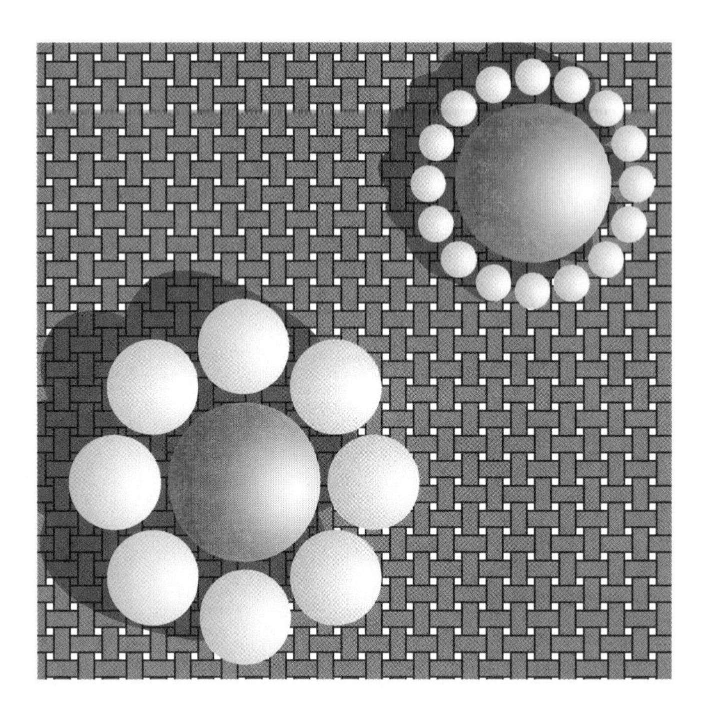

On first inspection these two orange circles appear to be different sizes – but they are actually exactly the same! The surrounding circles trick your brain into falsely compensating for 'distance'.

DOUBLE ARC

These two arcs seem to be different heights, but they are both the same size!

It might also look like the right-hand curve bends more sharply, but both arcs truly are identical.

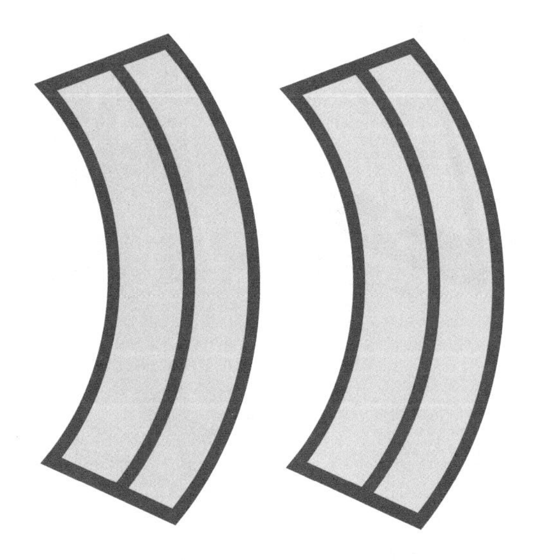

JUMP OUT

As you move your eyes around this strange, red image, it will appear to jump out at you in sharp, sudden forward leaps.

TRIPLE CREDIT

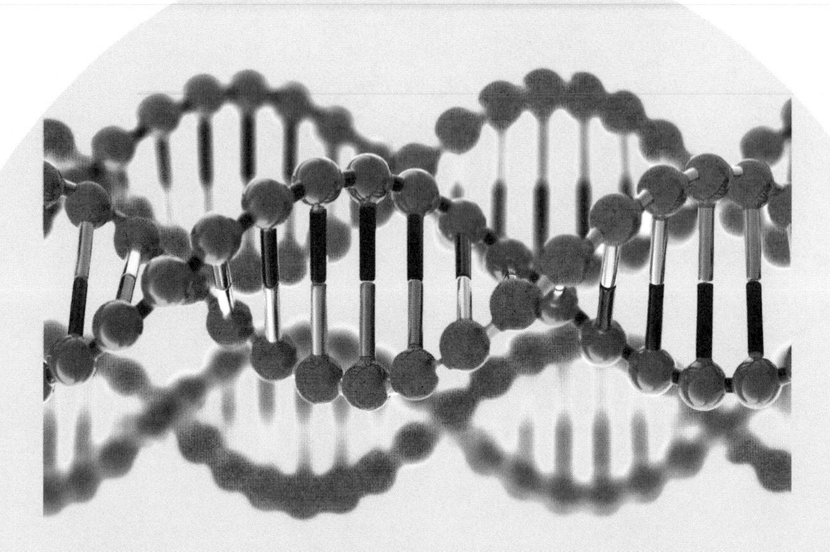

For many years, James Watson and Francis Crick have been jointly credited for the seminal discovery of the double-helix structure of DNA in the early 1950s, and they were awarded a Nobel Prize for the discovery in 1962, along with their supervisor, Maurice Wilkins. In reality, Rosalind Franklin was also a key part of the breakthrough but, arguably due to her gender, and perhaps also due to her premature death in 1958, she has only recently received full recognition for her contribution to this remarkable breakthrough.

GREEN OR GREY?

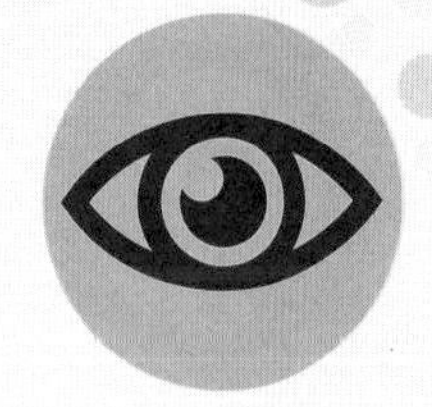

This cat appears to have two green eyes, but it's an optical illusion. If you look closely, the eye on the left is actually completely grey. The surrounding purple hue is responsible for this effect.

CATS' EYES

Cats need only one eighth of the light that humans do in order to be able to see, thanks to their elliptical pupils, which they can narrow to a slit during the day to provide much better control over extremes of light. They also have larger lenses than humans, and a reflective layer that increases the relative brightness within the cat's eye – and which can make their eyes appear to glow in the dark!

EXTRA SQUARE

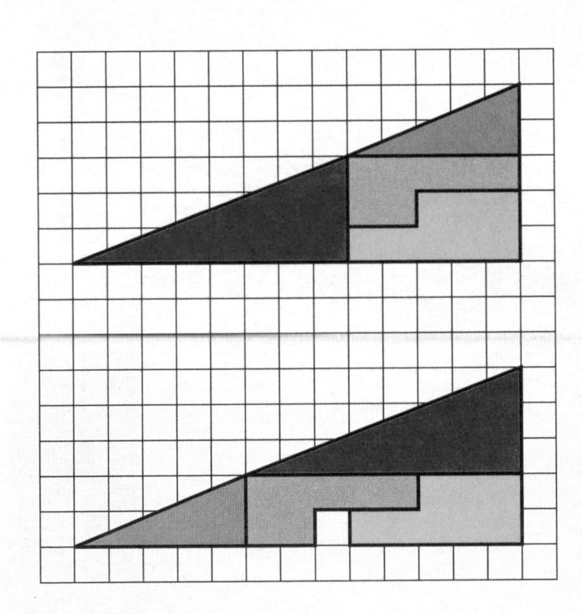

The outer triangle in the top image is cut up as shown and then rearranged as per the bottom picture. When this is done an extra space appears, as shown – you can try this with a bit of paper to prove it to yourself!

SLIPPERY RECTANGLES

These rectangles seem to slide around the page, simply just by looking at them!

STEAM MACHINE

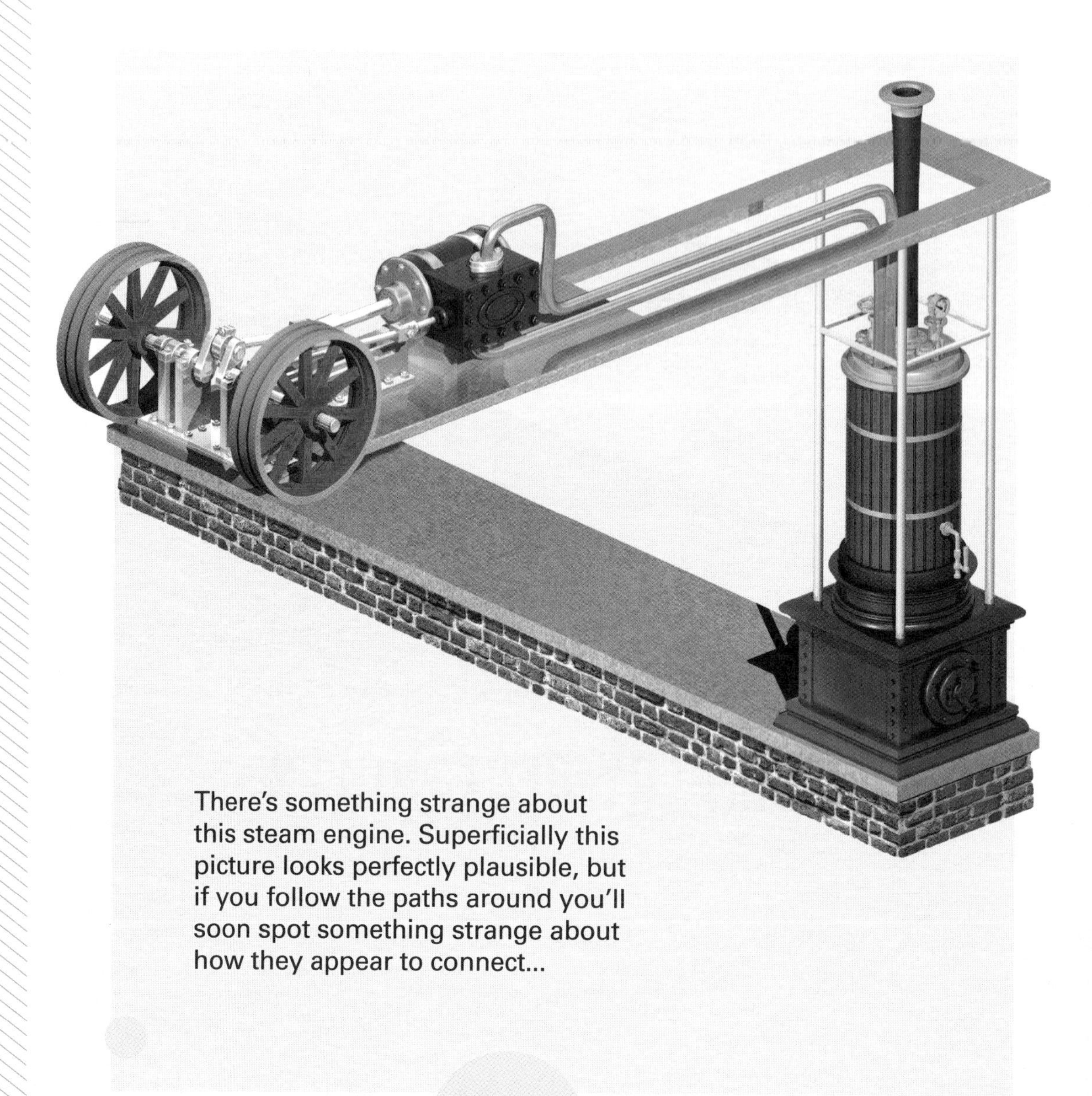

There's something strange about this steam engine. Superficially this picture looks perfectly plausible, but if you follow the paths around you'll soon spot something strange about how they appear to connect...

WORLDWIDE WONDER

The highest natural temperature ever recorded on the surface of the Earth was observed in Death Valley, California, in 1913. Weather instruments recorded a temperature of 56.7 °C (134 °F).

By contrast, the lowest natural temperature ever recorded was in Antarctica in 1983, when a surface temperature of -89.2°C (-128.6°F) was reached.

BIG EYES

Tarsiers are small primates with enormous eyes – so large, in fact, that they have the largest eyes of any mammal in relation to their body size, and indeed each eyeball is individually as large as the animal's brain! They are also unable to move their eyeballs, but compensate for this by being able to turn their head by 180 degrees.

WHAT DO YOU SEE?

At first glance this seems to be half a face facing forwards. Or is it actually half a face viewed side-on?

BLACK AND WHITE

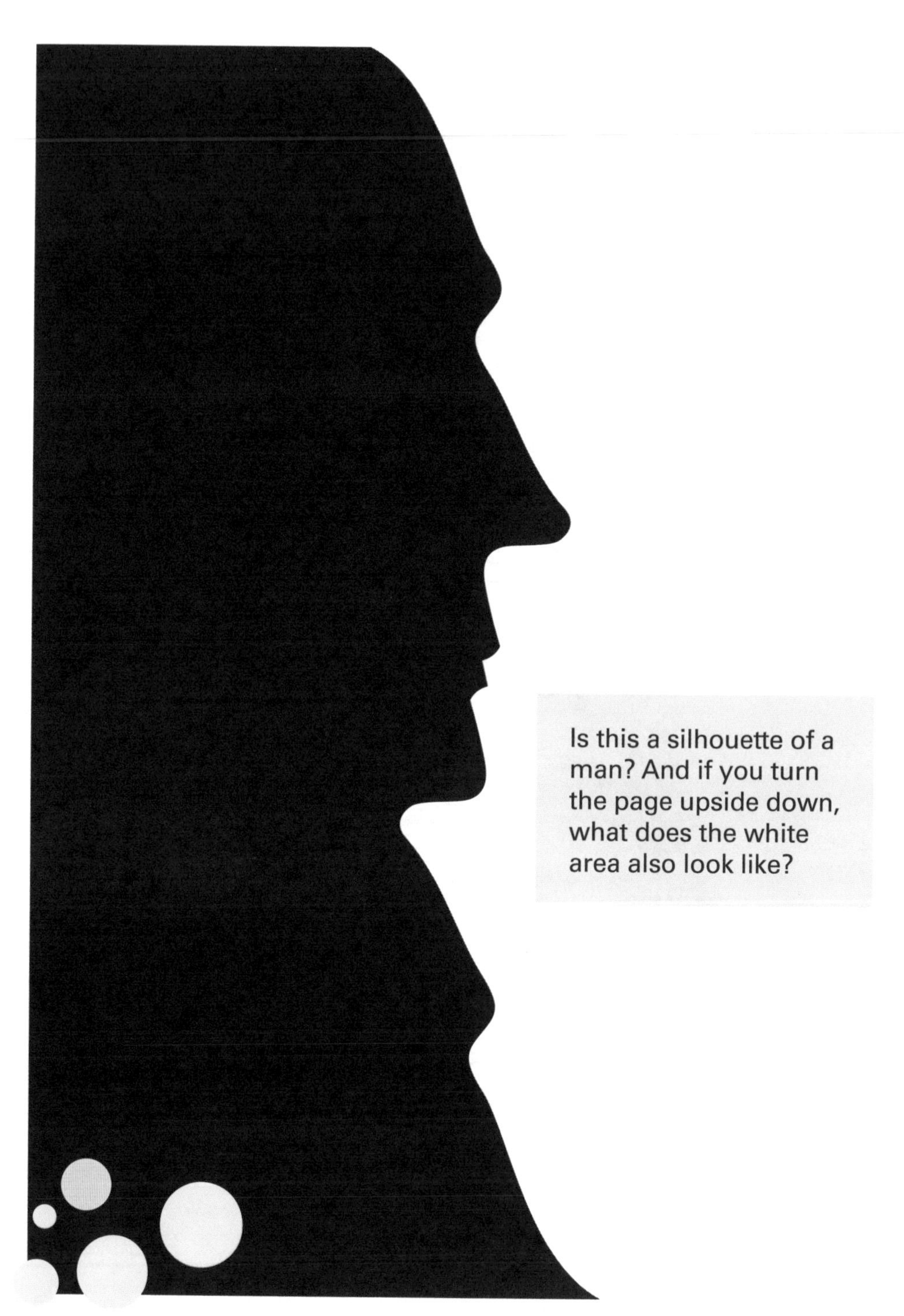

Is this a silhouette of a man? And if you turn the page upside down, what does the white area also look like?

MOVE TO THE RHYTHM

Move your eyes around the image below and you'll see it sway, bulge and move in all kinds of unexpected ways! Your brain seems to be trying to straighten the curves, and is confused by the strongly contrasting colours.

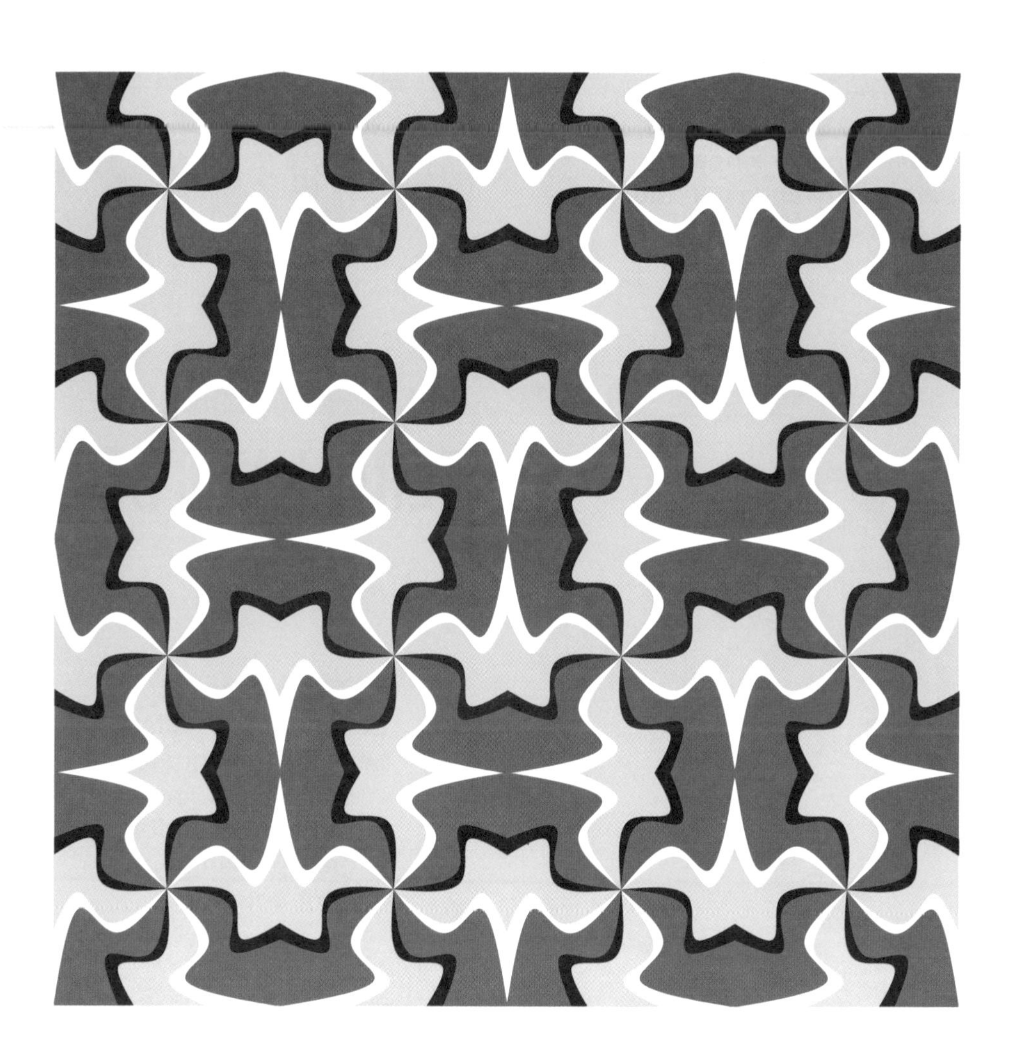

MANY REINDEER

The Sami language of Finland, Norway and Sweden has a very large number of different words for 'reindeer'. There are around 1,000 of them, in fact! The different words embody such concepts as a reindeer's health, personality and even the shape of its antlers.

ZERO LATITUDE

The country of Ecuador is so-called because the equator passes straight through it. 'Ecuador' is the Spanish word for equator.

FLOATING BLUR

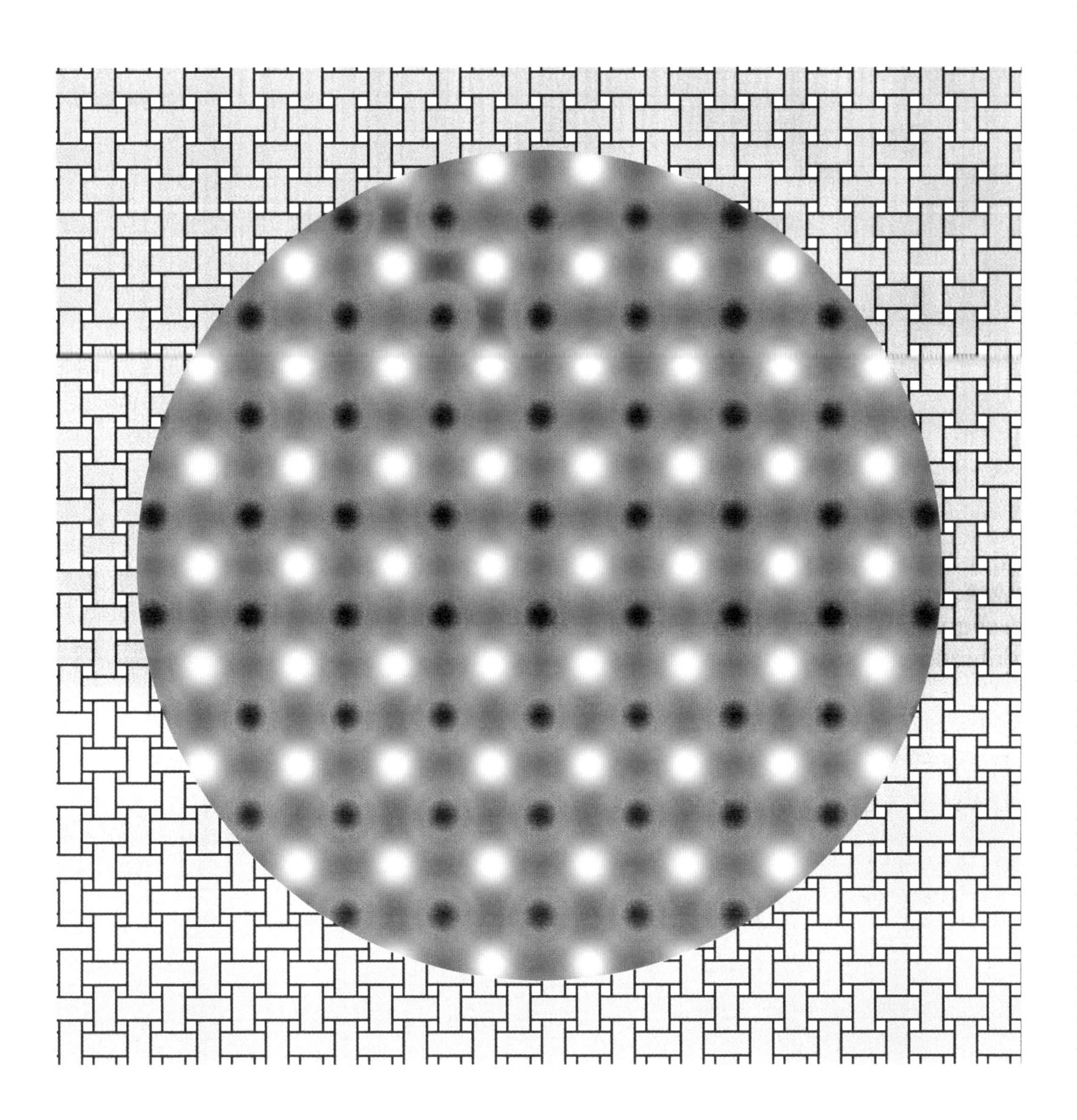

Focus on the blurred circle above, then let your eyes go slightly out of focus. Does it look like the circle starts to float above the background? This is due to the strong contrast in the visual clarity of the two surfaces.

QWERTY WORDS

'Typewriter' is often claimed to be the longest word that can be spelt using a single row of a regular QWERTY keyboard. While there seems not to be any longer word, 'typewriter' is not unique – there's also 'perpetuity', 'prerequire', 'proprietor' and 'repertoire'.

TITAN SNAKE

Fifty-eight million years ago, the lowland tropics of Colombia were home to the giant snake Titanoboa, each more than 12 m (40 ft) long and weighing more than 900 kg (1 ton). The thickest part of the snake reached almost 1 m (3.2 ft) above the ground.

DON'T LOOK AWAY...

The alternating colours in this pattern make it very hard to look at, encouraging you to look away!

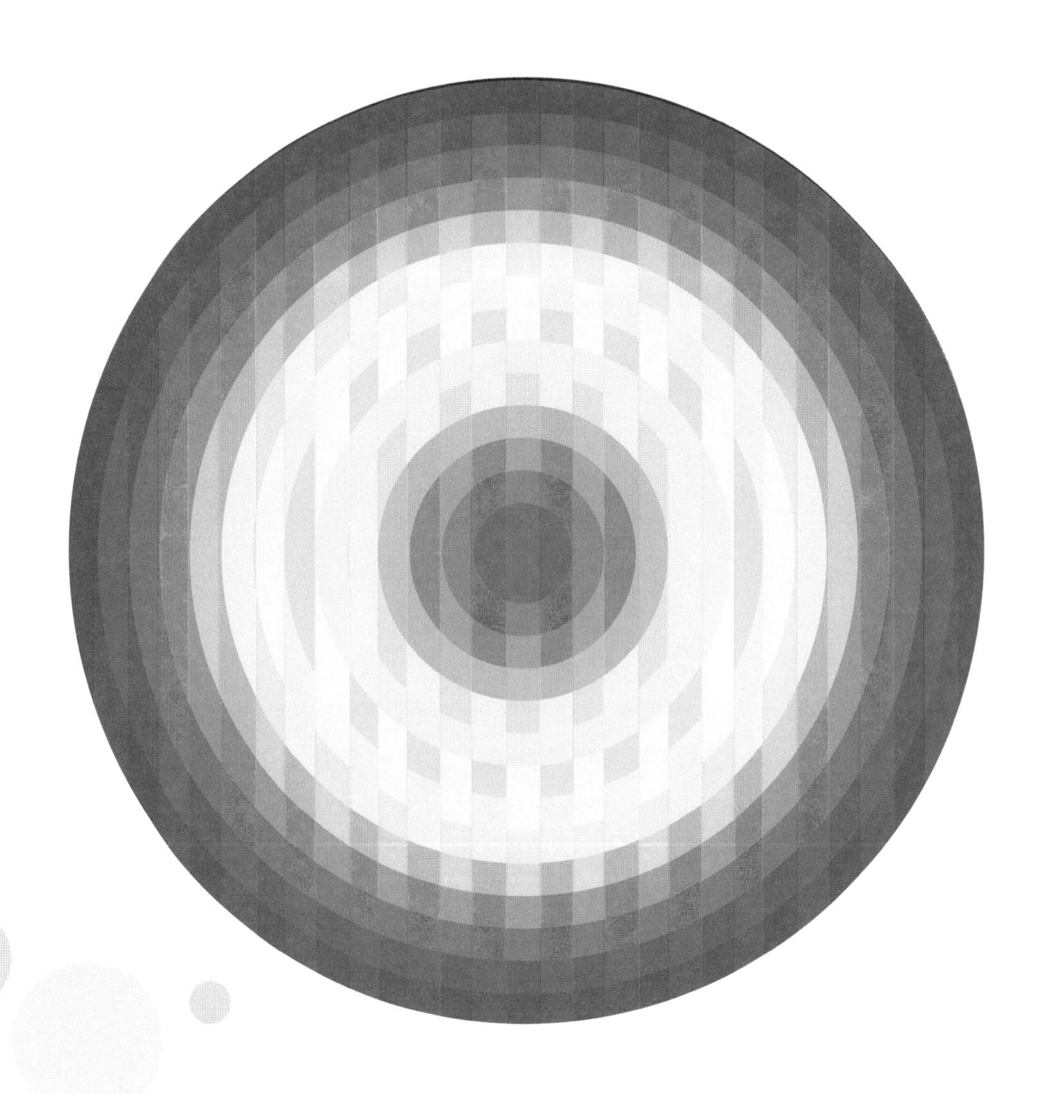

ANIMAL ANTICS

Flamingos can only feed when their head is upside down, which is why their jaws and tongue are reversed compared to other birds.

Some animals appear to have four knees, but in fact the 'front knees' in animals such as the elephant are actually wrists. Most mammals have essentially the same skeletal structure as humans.

FLOATING LAYERS

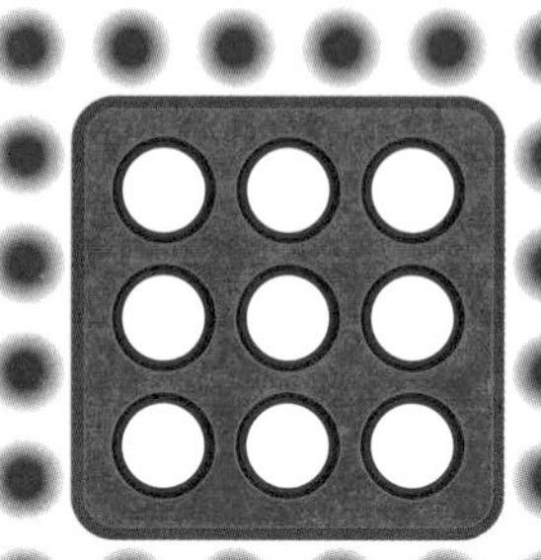

This central red shape appears to float on a higher layer than the black circles surrounding it. This is due to the huge variation in clarity between the two layers.

COG CONNECTION

What would happen if you tried to turn the upper cog? Could you actually make this mechanism in reality?

The truth is that you could never build this – the metal frame is impossible, even without considering the cogs.

SEVEN OVER FIVE

Isaac Newton originally divided the rainbow into five colours: red, yellow, green, blue and violet. He later added orange and indigo out of the belief that seven was a universal fundamental number: seven days, seven classical Greek 'planets' (Sun, Moon, Mercury, Venus, Mars, Jupiter, Saturn), and seven musical notes (A–G).

The frustrations of generations of children who have struggled to understand the seemingly arbitrary difference between indigo and violet are reflected by contemporary colour scientists who simply exclude indigo altogether from the colour spectrum. Indeed, studies of Newton's work indicate that the colour he called 'indigo' should properly be called 'blue', and his 'blue' would then more properly be called 'cyan'.

SPIRAL WONDER

This appears to be a drawing of a spiral, winding ever closer to the centre of the image. But if you put your finger on the spiral and trace it round the picture, you'll discover that it's actually a series of concentric circles – the spiral is completely illusory!

JUGGLING BALLS

This juggler has a lot of spheres in the air! Luckily they're only rotating slowly, as you can see if you look at them on the page...

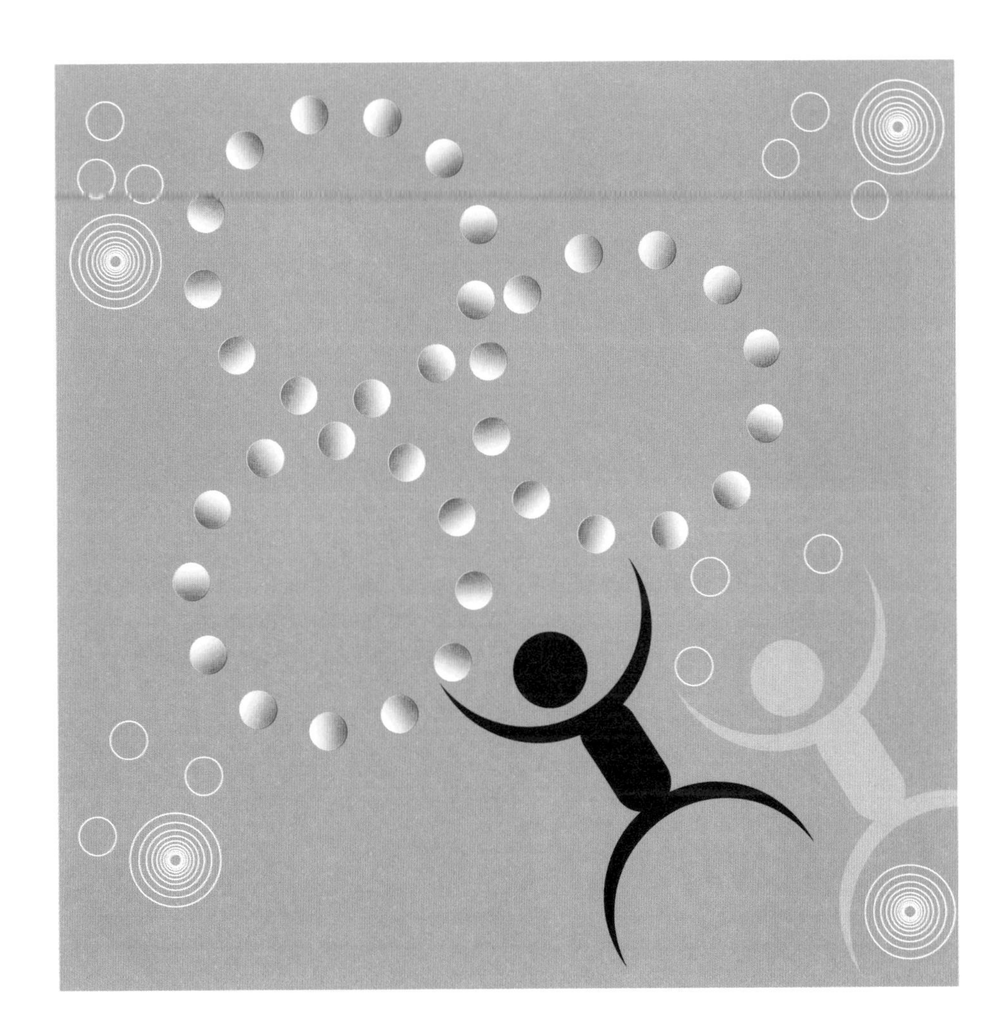

SPACE ROTATIONS

Most of the planets rotate on their axis in an anticlockwise direction, the same as the Sun. The two exceptions are Venus and Uranus, which rotate in the opposite direction. All of the planets orbit the Sun in an anticlockwise direction, however.

CLEAN WATER?

When the water in a chlorinated swimming pool gets dirtier, the intensity of the chlorine smell will increase. It is therefore best to avoid pools with very strong smells!

MINUTE MOVES

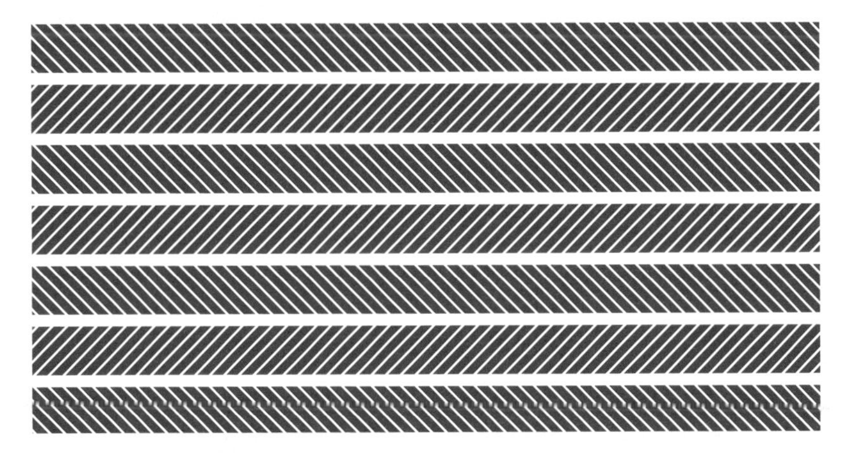

Do you see flickering dots and movement along the thick white lines? This is purely a figment of your imagination!

INVISIBLE DOTS

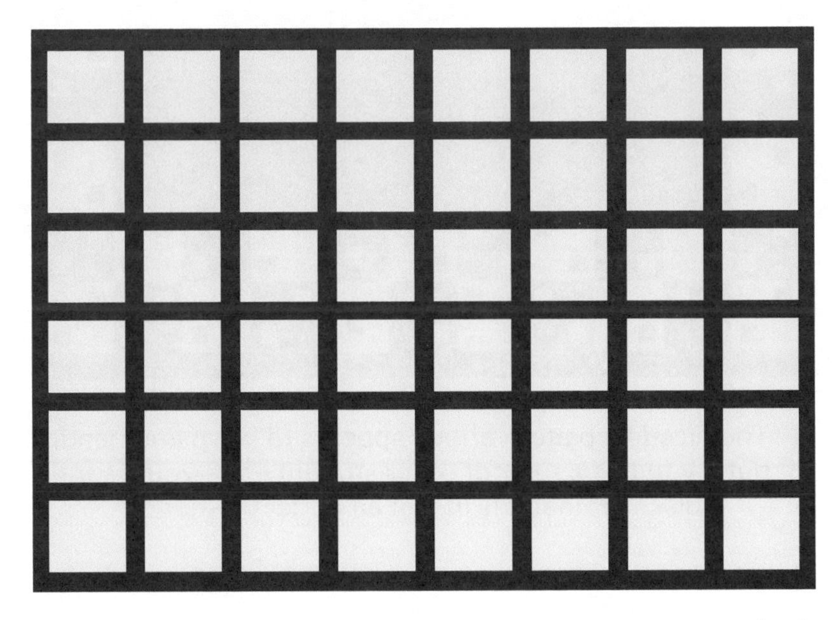

This scintillating grid effect, where dots seem to appear in the grid intersections, is called the Hermann Grid after its discovery in the 19th century by German scientist Ludimar Hermann.

STRAIGHT OR BENDY?

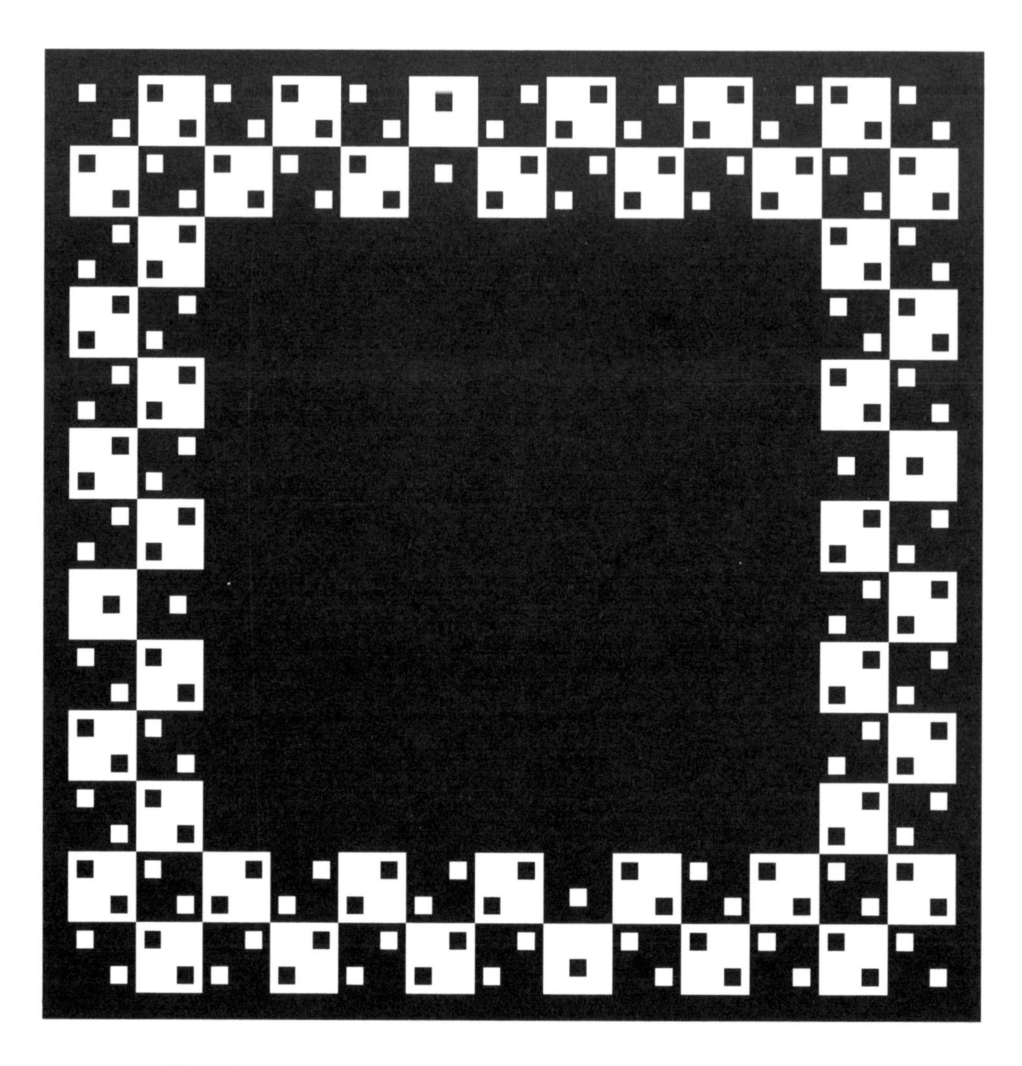

The dice-like pattern above appears to warp and bend, but if you use a ruler or other straight edge you'll soon discover that it is in fact all perfectly square!

WEIGHT PROBLEM

Vultures sometimes eat so much food that they become too heavy to take off, so if they need to do so to escape a predator they will vomit their food back out of their stomach. It has been claimed that they also vomit on attackers as a direct and deliberate act of defence, but this is not true.

THAI DOWN

It's illegal to go out in public in Thailand unless you're wearing underwear. It's also illegal to step on any Thai currency, since it bears the King's picture.

EXTINCT SPECIES

No one can be absolutely certain because we don't know exactly how many species are on the planet, but scientists estimate that we lose somewhere between 10,000 and 100,000 species of life every year to extinction. This is between 1,000 and 10,000 times the natural extinction rate that would be expected if humans weren't involved.

EASTER FOREST

The famous moai statues were carved on Easter Island between around AD 1250 and AD 1500. Pollen analysis has shown that the island was almost completely covered in forest in around AD 1200. By the time the first Europeans landed in 1722 the islanders had cut down all of the trees that once grew on the island, leaving it as an entirely treeless place. This therefore provides an early example of accidental environmental destruction!

IT'S IN HAND

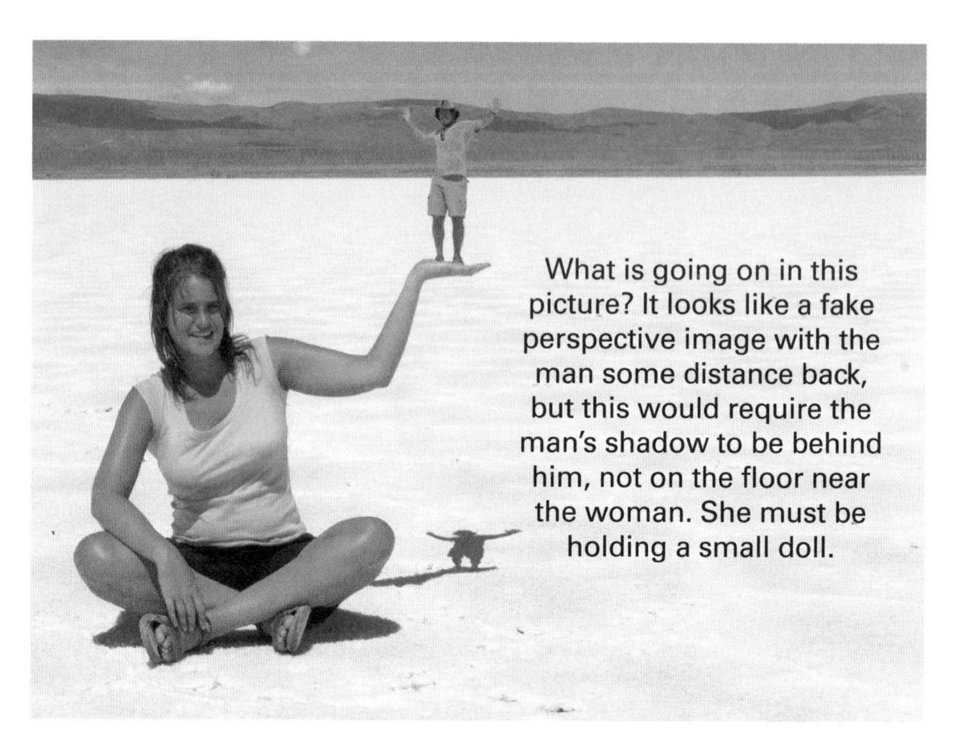

What is going on in this picture? It looks like a fake perspective image with the man some distance back, but this would require the man's shadow to be behind him, not on the floor near the woman. She must be holding a small doll.

SHADES OF GREEN

Cover over the parts of this image outside the dashed lines and all four green segments seem to be the same colour, but as you can see when you uncover it, they are in fact different shades!

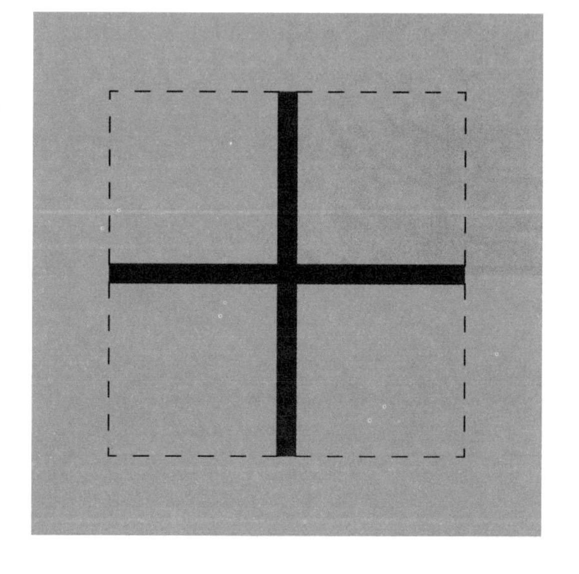

EARLY COKE

Coca-Cola® was originally intended to be used as a medicine, when it was first introduced in the late 19th century by its inventor, pharmacist John Pemberton (1831–1888).

LARGE FRUIT

A pumpkin is actually a fruit, albeit a very large one, since it grows from the flowering part of the plant. On the same basis, tomatoes, peas, beans, sweetcorn, aubergine and peppers are also all fruit, botanically speaking.

MAD SHAPES

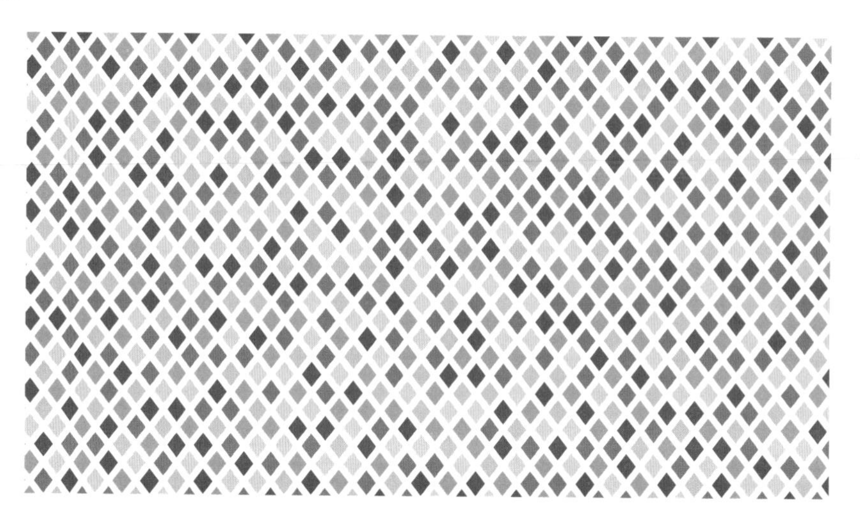

The image above consists of randomly coloured diamonds, but your brain can't help but see patterns and even shapes in it. Your vision system likes to try to make sense of whatever you give it.

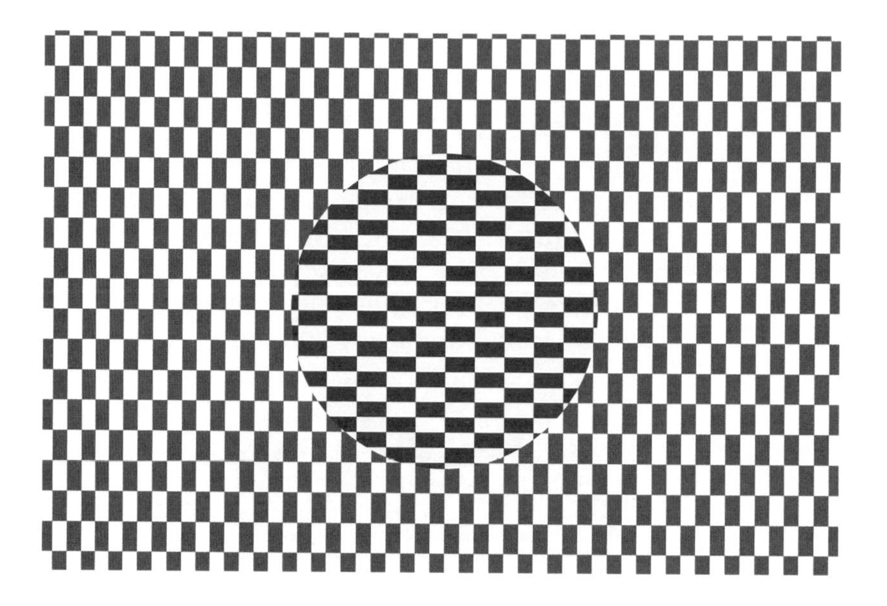

Move the book back and forth from left to right and then right to left. Does the circle above appear to float on top of the background?

COUNT YOUR BEANS

Beethoven was very particular about his coffee, and would hand count exactly 60 beans when making each cup he drank!

SWAN UPPING

The British Crown has had the right to claim ownership of all unmarked wild swans found in open water since the 12th century. The Queen continues to exercise this right only on the River Thames and its tributaries, however. Each year a Swan Upping ceremony takes place to record and label all of the swans in the area.

FLOATING SQUARES

Do these squares appear to be rotating
around the centre of the image?

SHORT TERM

William Henry Harrison, who became President of the USA in 1841, died after just a month in office, possibly having caught pneumonia during his inauguration speech, by giving the longest-such speech ever made. Delivered in the pouring rain, without a coat, it took him two hours to read the speech. He therefore served the shortest term of any USA president in history, at just 30 days, 12 hours and 30 minutes! He was also the first president of the USA to die while in office.

FETCH THE KETCHUP

Over 650 million bottles of Heinz® Ketchup are sold each year, in over 140 different countries. In addition, two single-serve sachets of ketchup are sold each year per person on the planet!

TIME FOR TEA

The teabag was invented in the USA in 1908, by Thomas Sullivan, a New York tea merchant. It was an accidental invention, since he originally put the tea in the bags simply as a means of preparing samples, but due to confusion over their usage the teabag was born!

LEANING SHAPES

The image to the left is a perfect rectangle, believe it or not, and all of the shapes within it are square. It looks like the grid lines are diagonal, but if you use a straight edge you'll see that they're all completely horizontal or vertical.

VERTICAL DEPTH

The height of the lines in the image to the right seem to vary as you travel along the wave, but in fact each of the vertical bars is precisely the same height!

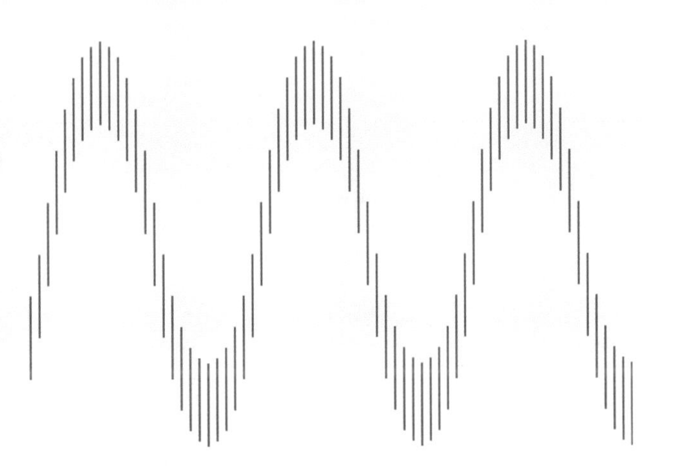

CATS AND DOGS

The phrase 'raining cats and dogs' is of uncertain provenance, but its most likely explanation is a reference to the lack of waste disposal facilities in early industrial Britain, when dead animals would literally wash down the road during heavy rain.

TRIPLE DOUBLE

The only English word which has three repeated letters in a row is

'bookkeeper'.

STARE AT THE STAIR

This seems to be a modern-looking stair installation, but there's something wrong with these green steps. Although they appear to make sense, if you trace around the upper level of the grey blocks you'll see that this arrangement couldn't be built in reality.

SQUARES OR CIRCLES?

The pattern to the left appears to contain glowing white circles, but in fact only straight lines are present. Even without the diagonal lines, the effect remains.

WAYWARD GRID

This image appears to consist of a curved mesh, but once again all of the grid lines run in straight horizontal or vertical lines across the image.

DOT FOCUS

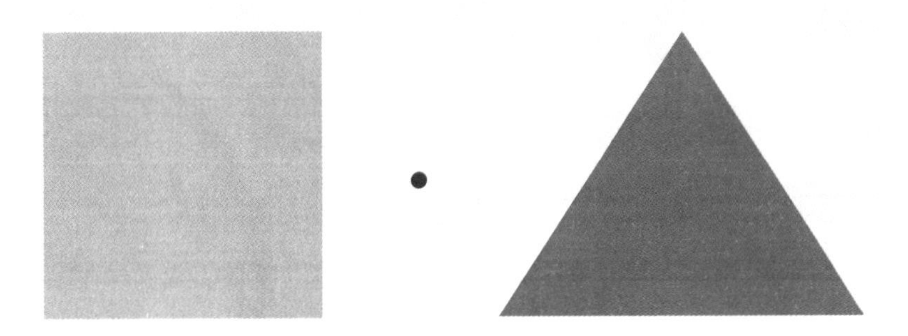

Stare at the dot in the centre of the upper image for 30 seconds, then rapidly transfer your focus to the corresponding dot in the lower image. You should briefly see the grey shapes change to a green square and red triangle on top of a yellow background.

FOOD OF THE GODS

Chocolate is derived from the cocoa tree, Theobroma cacao. This name comes from the Greek for 'food of the gods.' The earliest known evidence of chocolate consumption dates to 1900 BC, in an area that is now part of Mexico.

STAR SUCCESS

George Lucas was so sure that the original *Star Wars* movie would be a failure that he went on holiday instead of attending the film's premiere. He only realized its success, and his sudden personal wealth, when he saw the evening news on TV!

SUPER LONG PLACE

The longest single-word place name in Britain is the Welsh place name

Llanfairpwllgwyngyllgogerychwyrn-drobwllllantysiliogogogoch

which translates from its original Welsh as 'St. Mary's Church in the hollow of the white hazel near the rapid whirlpool of Llantysilio of the red cave'. This is a bit of a mouthful for locals, so they tend to refer to it by a range of shorter names, including 'Llanfair PG'. The long name was originally chosen in the 1860s as a publicity stunt to attract visitors.

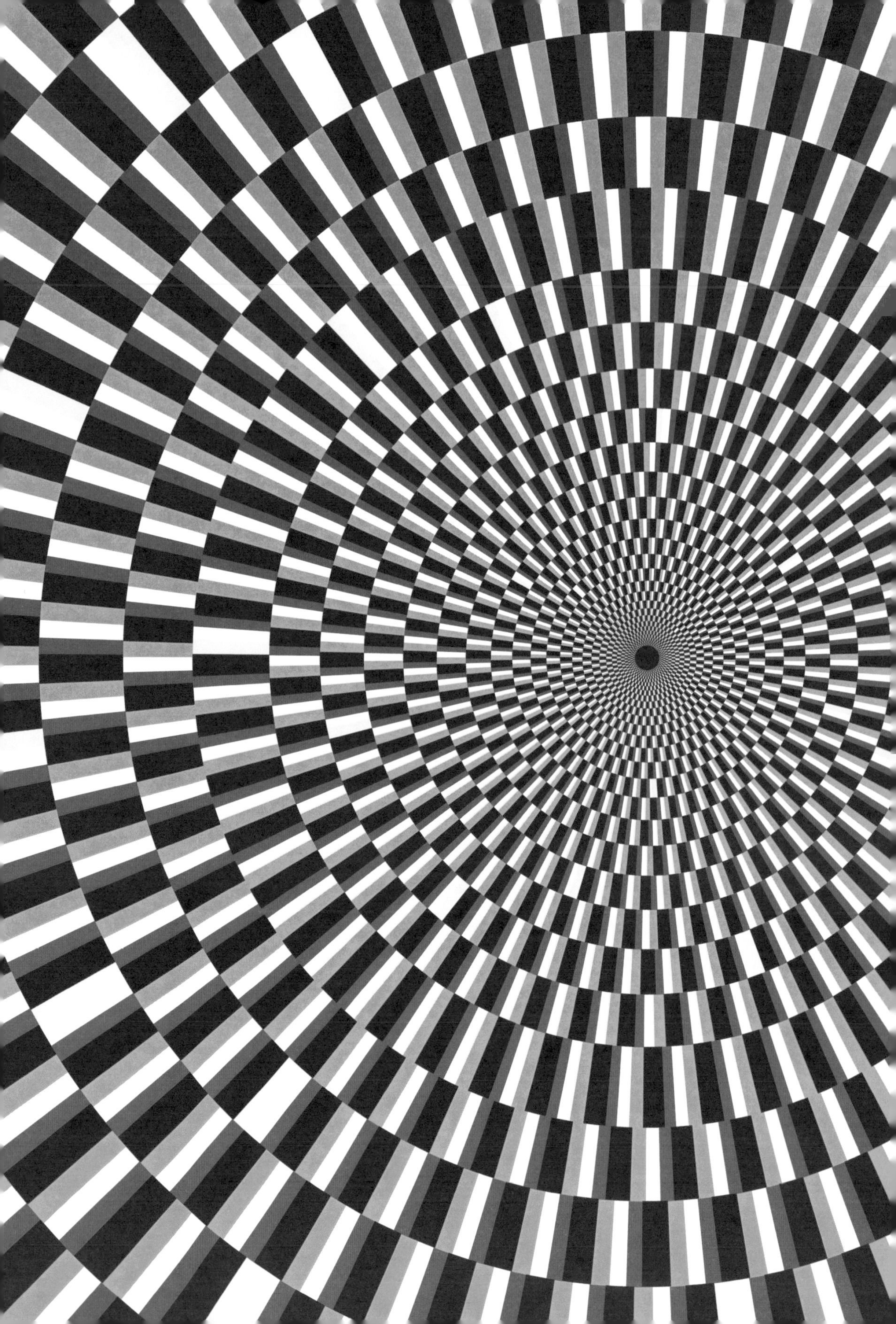

SPIRAL HYPNOTISM

The centre of this image
really does seem to shake with a
nervous energy – as if trying to turn,
yet not quite managing to move.

FEED THE BIRDS

Pigeons can remember humans by face, and will quickly learn to seek out those that feed them – and to avoid those who harass them!

STAR STRUCK

As of 2017, there have been six *Star Trek* television series and 13 *Star Trek* films, as well as a much larger number of video games, novels and comics. Ironically the original series was cancelled after just three seasons.

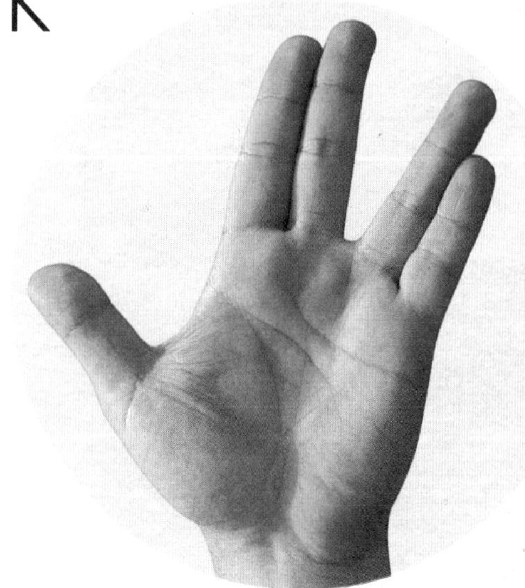

NORMAL FACE?

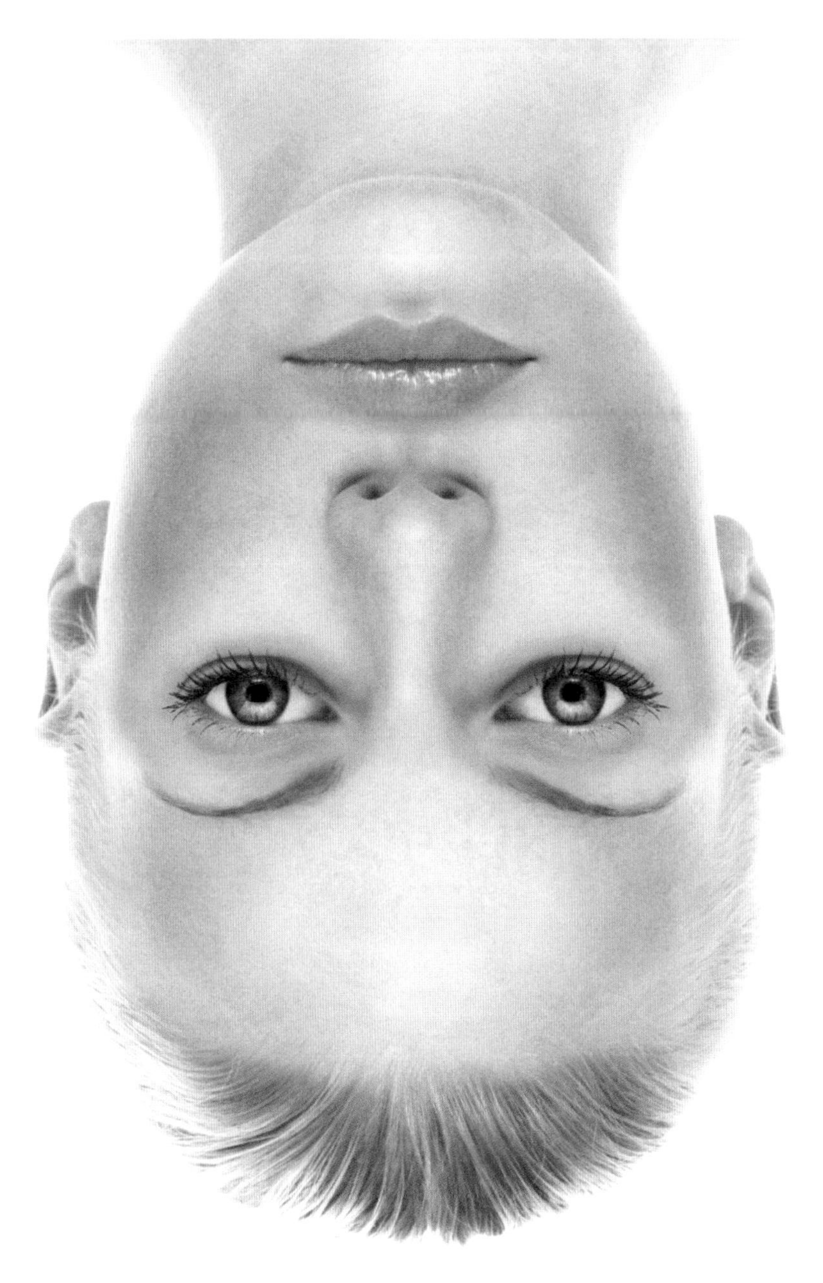

This image looks perfectly normal, apart from being upside down. Now try turning the book upside down instead. Does it still look normal?

EXPANDING SPECIES

New species are being discovered all the time. For example, in just one forest in Panama, in just 19 trees, scientists discovered 960 new species of beetle, back in 1980. The chances are that we have only so far identified one or two per cent of all species on Earth.

FORBIDDEN PIE

It is often said that the British statute book once forbade eating mince pies on Christmas Day, but in fact this was strictly speaking only the case in 1644. Parliament had enacted legislation that mandated days of fasting, which in that year included Christmas Day, and so food such as mince pies could not be consumed. Mince pies were not themselves explicitly banned, however.

PATH ILLUSION

These two path shapes appear to lean at very different angles, but take a closer look and you'll see that in fact they are identical! This remarkable illusion works thanks to your brain's auto-correction for the contents of what it assumes must be a real-world view.

ON THE MOVE

These spiky shapes will start to swirl as you move your eyes diagonally across the page. This effect is caused entirely by the colour gradation on each shape.

FIRST CROSSWORD

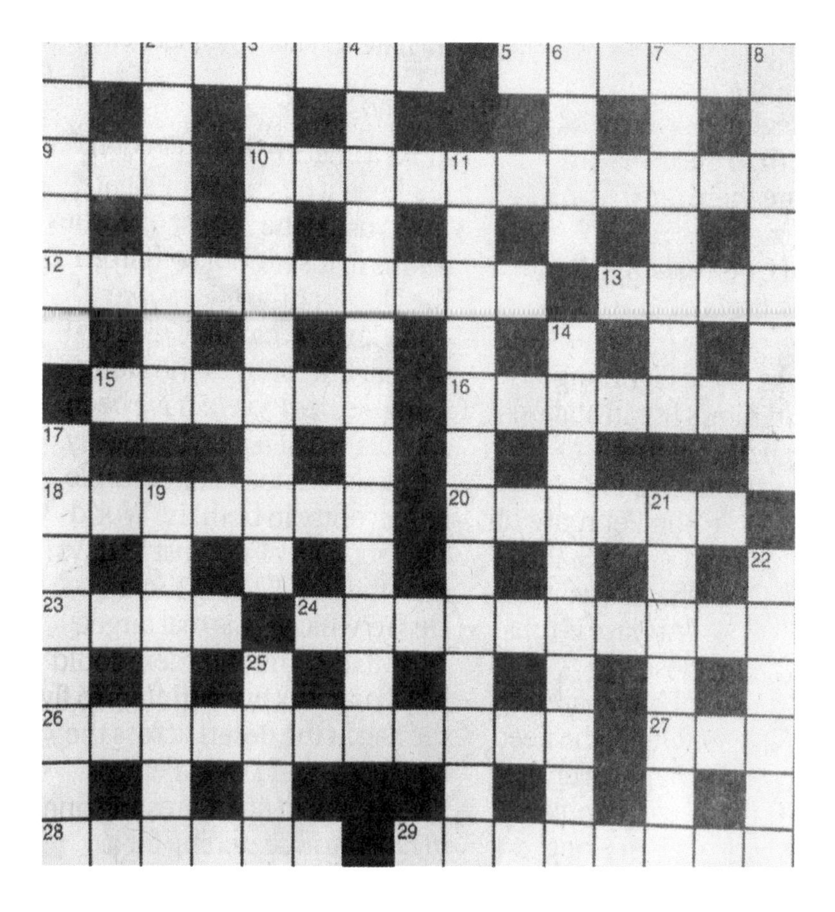

The first crossword was published in the USA in 1913 in the *New York World*. It was called 'Word-Cross' and had a simple diamond-shaped grid. Crosswords were not introduced to the UK until 1922, but when eventually the *London Times* gave in to demand in 1930 and began to publish the puzzle, it also published a Latin version, describing the English-language puzzle as failing to meet its 'exacting intellectual standard'.

CHEQUERED BALLS

As you move your eyes around this picture, so the balls appear to shift and start to jostle for space on the page.

If you're having trouble seeing the illusion, try looking away and then rapidly shifting your gaze back. Another method is to look at the centre, let your eyes go slightly out of focus, then move them around the image in that soft-focus state.

THREE SILHOUETTES

Does the silhouette on the far right of this image look larger than the silhouette on the left? It's an optical illusion, caused by the background grid.

FAIR AND SQUARE?

This square appears to warp in towards the centre of the circles, but in reality it is a perfect square with completely straight sides!

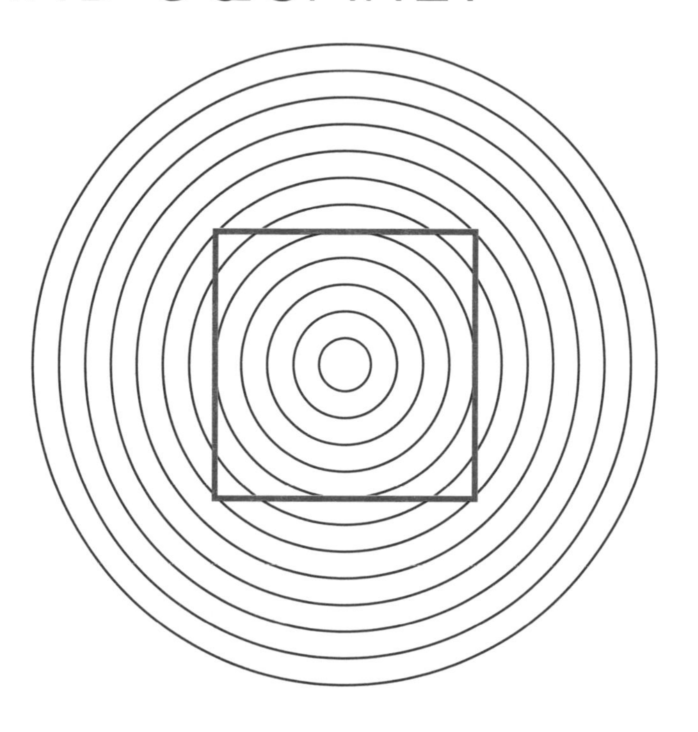

TUNNEL VISION

These black and white shapes give the impression of a tunnel of infinite length, burrowing down into the page. They also shimmer and distort towards the distant part of the tunnel!

GLOWING WHITE

The area inside this shape appears to be a brighter white than the white background outside the shape, but in fact this is an illusion – they are both the same colour.

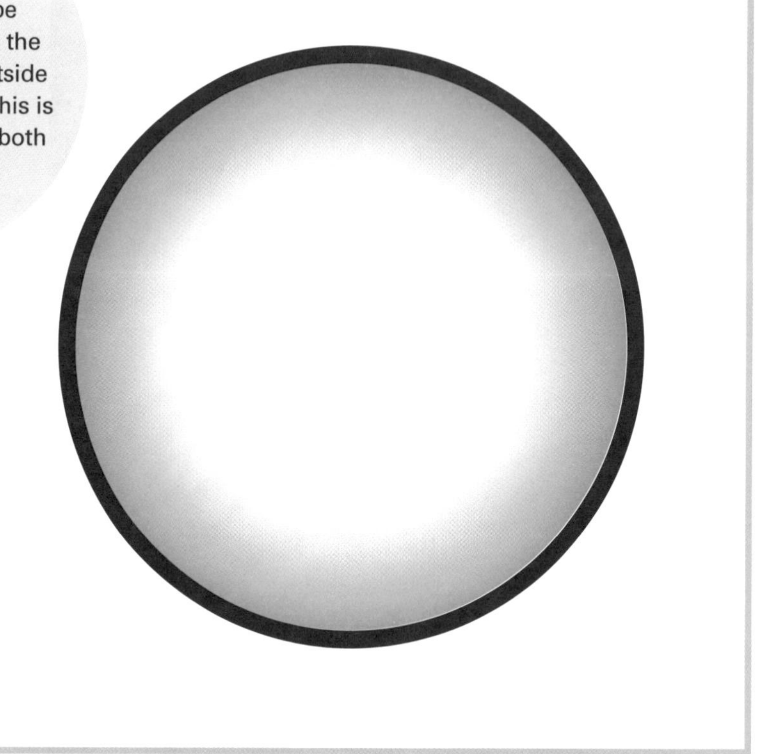

GRADUATED SPACES

The gaps between these posts seem to get narrower from left to right, but in fact each gap is exactly the same width!

BIG FUNGUS

The largest living organism on Earth is the honey fungus. A specimen in the Blue Mountains in Oregon, USA has been measured at up to 2.4 miles (3.8 km) across. Mushrooms from the fungus appear above ground, but they are only the fruiting bodies of the much larger underground part of the organism.

ALL SHIP SHAPE?

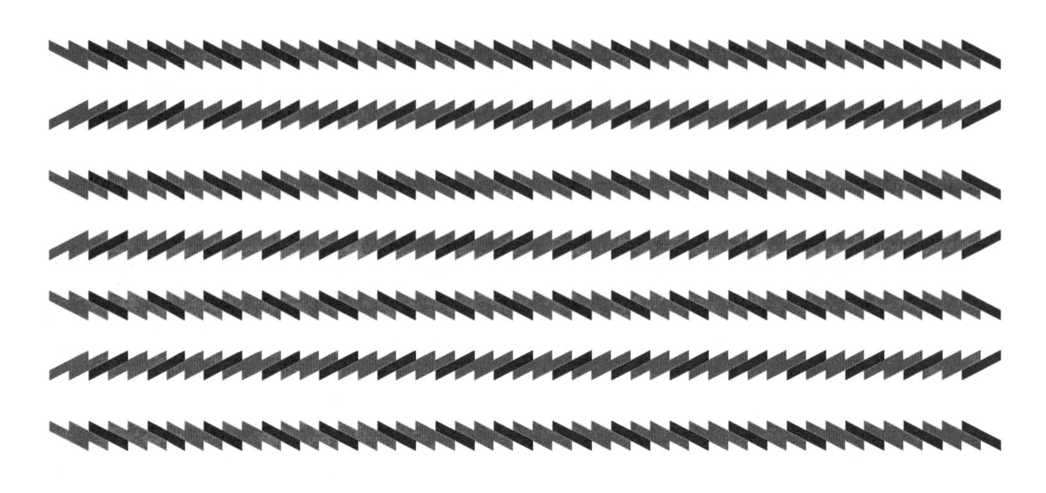

These rows of shapes appear to be angled, but are in fact completely straight.

BE HANDY

Is this a handprint – or is it a silhouette of two people?

If you look at the top first you'll see people, but if you look at the bottom first you'll see a hand!

SEAL OF APPROVAL

Each incoming President of the USA redecorates the Oval Office in the White House according to their own personal taste. Although the seal in the ceiling of the room remains constant, a new version of the Presidential Seal rug that forms one of the centrepieces of the room is designed for each president.

STILL A MYSTERY

The Mousetrap, a murder-mystery play by Agatha Christie, has run continuously in the West End theatre district of London since 1952. This makes it the longest continually running play in history.

TRUE COLOUR

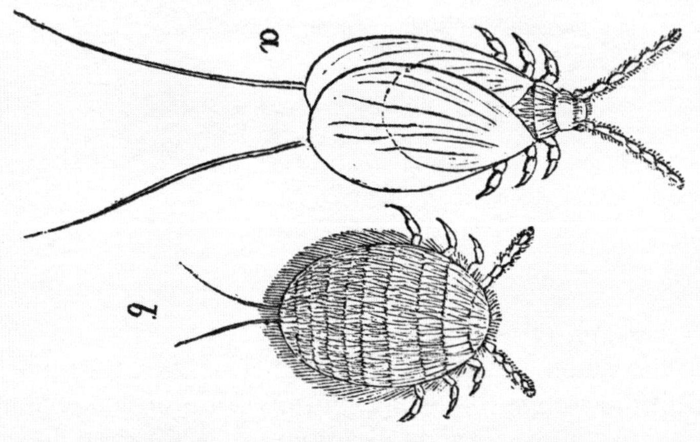

Red food colouring is traditionally made from the crushed cochineal insect, which produces a characteristic crimson-coloured dye. At one point manufacturing of the dye was reduced to small amounts due to the use of artificial alternatives, but with increased demand for 'natural' products the original dye is now once again being produced in large quantities.

WHITE FLARE

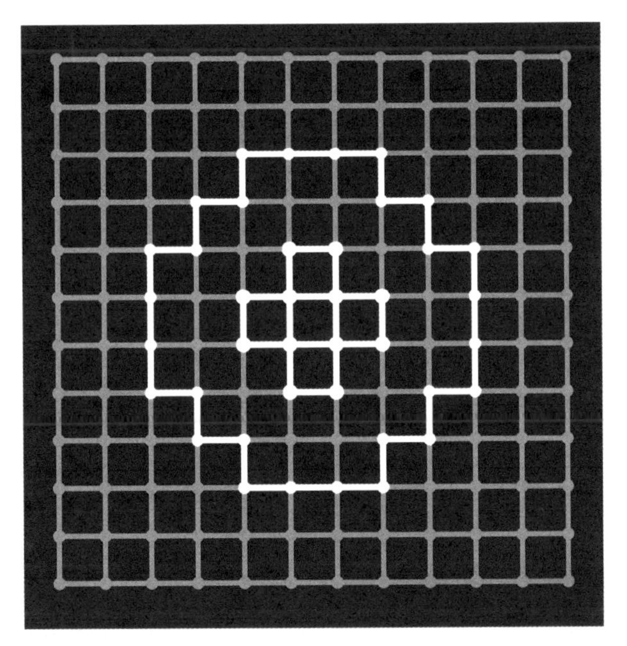

The areas around the white lines in this image seem to glow brighter than the rest of the page, but it's just an illusion.

CAN YOU SEE IT?

Can you spot the camouflaged bird in this picture? It's just left of centre, with its head raised up to the sky. This bird, a bittern, has subtle brown plumage that blends almost perfectly into its reed-bed habitat. When frightened, it stands perfectly still and points its beak upwards to look just like a reed stalk!

PLAYING WITH FIRE

What do you see when you look at this picture? Is it a yacht on a lake with a fire burning on a hill, or is it a ghostly blue face in the sky looking down on the Earth?

FAKE WORD

The longest word in any major English dictionary is

'pneumonoultramicroscopicsilicovolcanoconiosis',

although the word was actually invented in the 1930s as a fake word intended to imitate ridiculously long medical terms. Nonetheless, it appears in the Oxford English Dictionary.

Structural chemical compound names can be longer – one is 189,819 letters long – but they aren't considered proper 'words' by lexicographers and so don't appear in dictionaries.

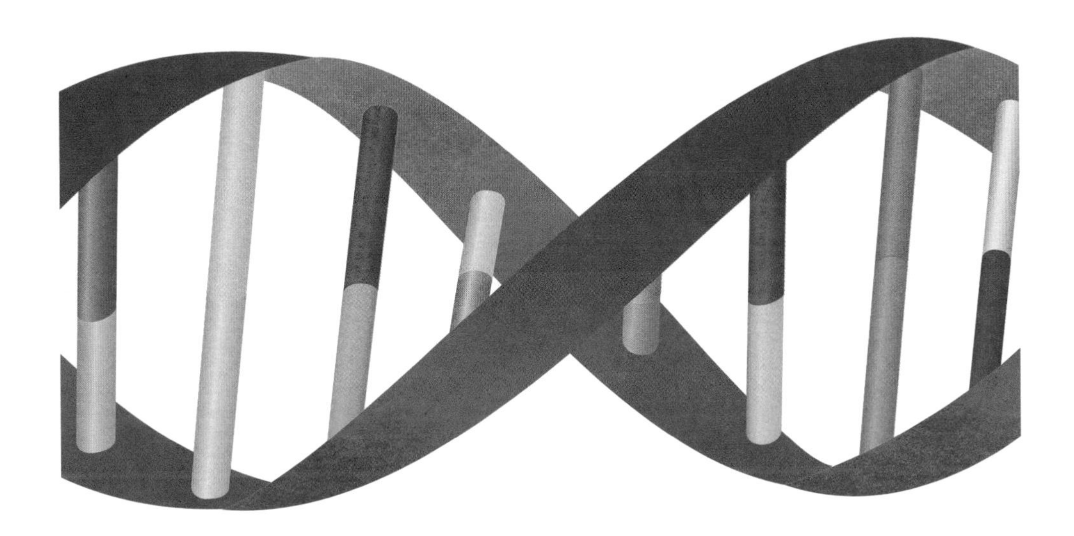

BRIDGE CHASM

This watery chasm has been created on this bridge using just chalk and an understanding of perspective.

TOW ON THE TOUR

In 1904, Hippolyte Aucouturier found a novel method to help him cycle the Tour de France – he used a car to tow himself along the road! Unlike some other competitors he did this during daylight hours and was seen and disqualified. The following year he finished second, presumably without cheating.

MEDAL CROP

The USA has won more medals in total at all Olympic Games than any other country – in fact it has more than double the number of medals of its nearest rival!

PLAY WELL

The LEGO® name is based on the first two letters of the Danish words, 'Leg godt', meaning 'play well'. Its founder, Ole Kirk Kristiansen, didn't know that in Latin it can be translated as 'I put together'!

LEGO® manufactures bricks at a rate of more than 117,000 elements every minute. That's more than 60 billion elements a year! If you laid all the bricks produced in a year end-to-end, they'd stretch more than 24 times around the world!

BAFFLING SHAPES

If you cut up a square as shown in the top image, then rearrange as per the image below, you end up with an extra piece sticking out. That's amazing! It's because the new shape is slightly less tall, so isn't really a square.

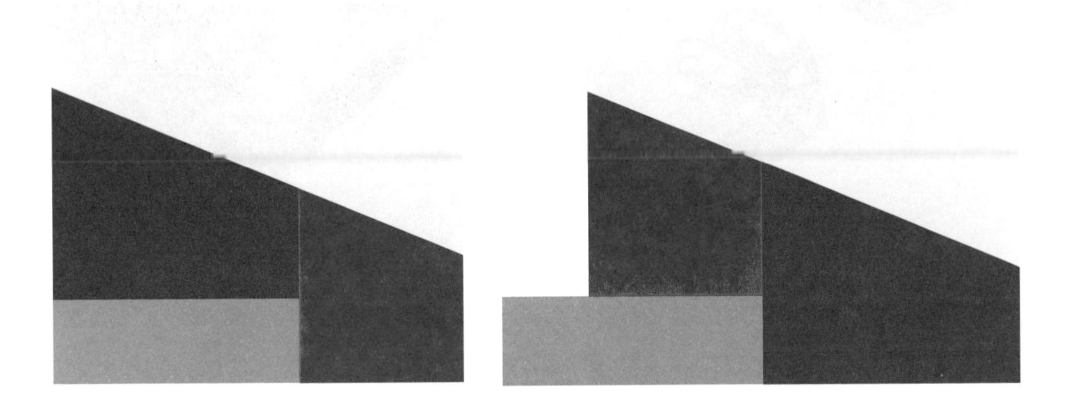

AFTER IMAGE

Stare at this black and white ring arrangement for 20 seconds, then look away at a white surface such as a wall. Do you see an inverted, ghostly after-image?

KEEP THE MONOPOLY

The popular board game, Monopoly®, was based on a 1904 game called The Landlord's Game, which was intended as an educational tool about private monopolies.

Monopoly® inspires such devotion that the longest-recorded game lasted an amazing 70 consecutive days, while the most expensive version of the game ever made featured a 23-carat-gold game board and diamond-encrusted dice! In 1941 the British intelligence service even used fake copies of the game to sneak items to prisoners of war.

CAN SQUIRRELS FLY?

The flying squirrel is unique among squirrels in being able to glide between trees, with flights of up to 90 m (295 ft). They do this by stretching out their 'patagium', a thin membrane that stretches between their wrist and ankle. Bats have a similar membrane. Other gliding mammals include the colugo, some species of possum and the anomaluridae – these last are also known as the 'scaly-tailed squirrel', but are not in fact 'true' squirrels.

SUCKED IN

Do you feel that you are getting sucked into the very centre of the book?

UPSTAIRS PUZZLE

This Escher-esque image would require some serious climbing skills if it existed in real life! Escher was a Dutch graphic artist, known for his illustrations that featured impossible architectural constructions.

GET CUBED

With Japanese households frequently short of physical space, some farmers now produce cube-shaped watermelons by growing them in glass boxes. This makes them easier to fit into fridges, and allows them to be stacked.

SPINNING DISCS

These flying saucers appear to spin as they travel through the air. This is due to the pattern of white and black markings on the discs.

TOP FILM STAR

John Wayne is the most successful leading man of all time, having had more lead roles in films than any other actor. He had top billing a staggering 142 times, and appeared in nearly 250 movies.

He appeared in more than 70 low-budget Westerns and other films before his first starring role in *Stagecoach* in 1939.

NOT EXTINCT

The Indonesian coelacanth fish, *Latimeria menadoensis*, was thought to have been extinct since the end of the Cretaceous period, 66 million years ago, until one was discovered alive in Indonesia in 1998.

NO BLACK TIE

During his time as James Bond, Pierce Brosnan was contractually forbidden from appearing on-screen in any other film while wearing black tie.

TWO TABLES

These tables look very different, but the green shapes are actually identical – you can measure them with a ruler to prove this!

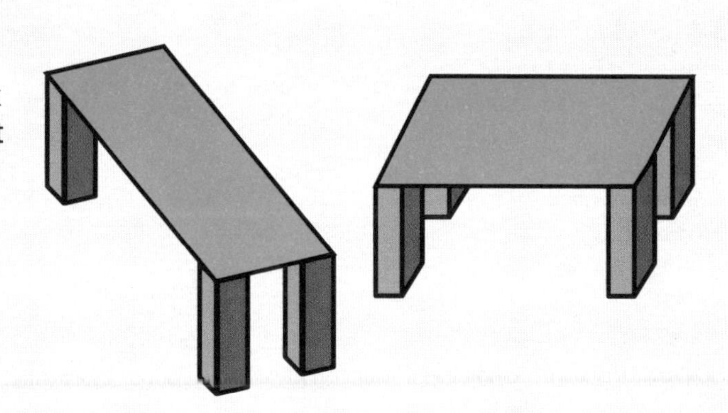

WHITER SHADES

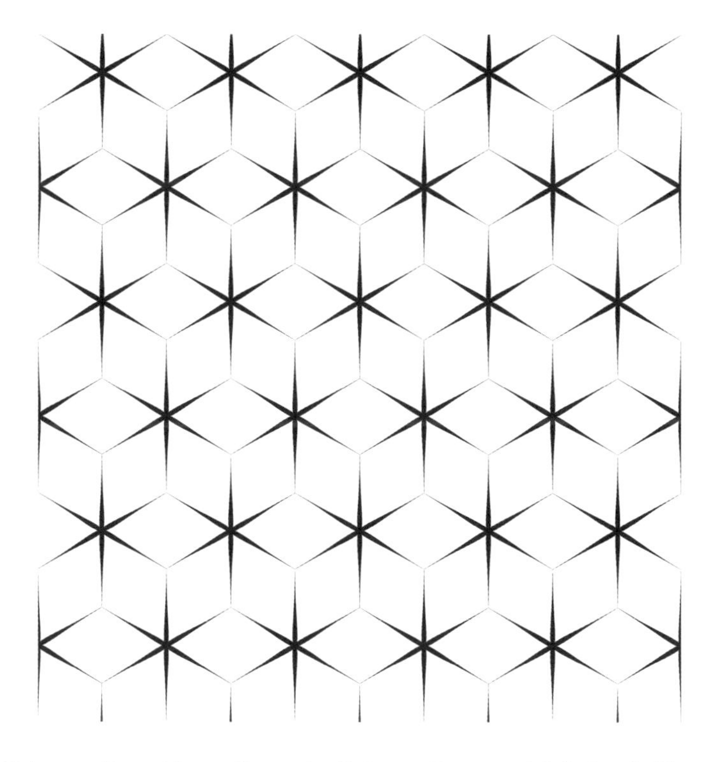

The thinner-lined junctions in this pattern, which look like a wall made of cubes, appear to glow slightly whiter than the paper colour. In fact, all the whites are the same shade.

COLOUR SHOW

Stare at the dot in the centre of the upper image for 30 seconds, then rapidly transfer your gaze to the black dot in the black and white image – which will now appear in colour!

INK SOURCE

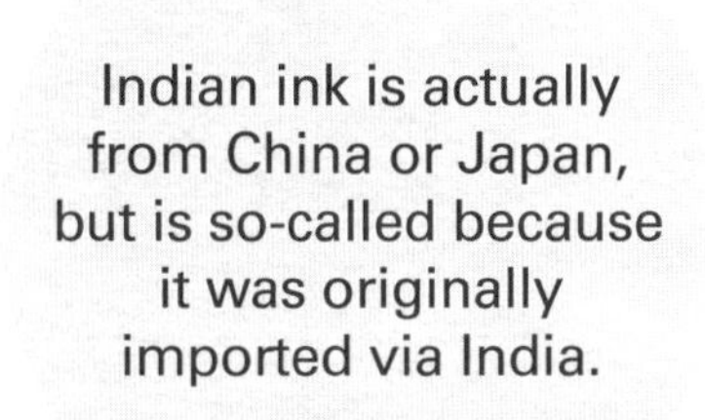

Indian ink is actually from China or Japan, but is so-called because it was originally imported via India.

CONTINENTAL SHIFT

Due to tectonic plate movement, the continent of America is moving ever further away from the continental land mass of Eurasia, at a rate of about 2.5 cm (1 in) per year. This means they are moving apart at about the same speed as which your fingernails grow.

SURROUNDING MOVES

As you look at the centre of one of these arrangements of blue shapes, so the three other ones will seem to rotate!

LOST CELLS

In the two years after puberty, the human brain loses an average of 5,000 brain cell connections per second! This massive spring clean tidies up the brain at the point when it thinks we have learnt all of the most important things, such as how to use language. Even after this process, around 100 trillion connections still remain!

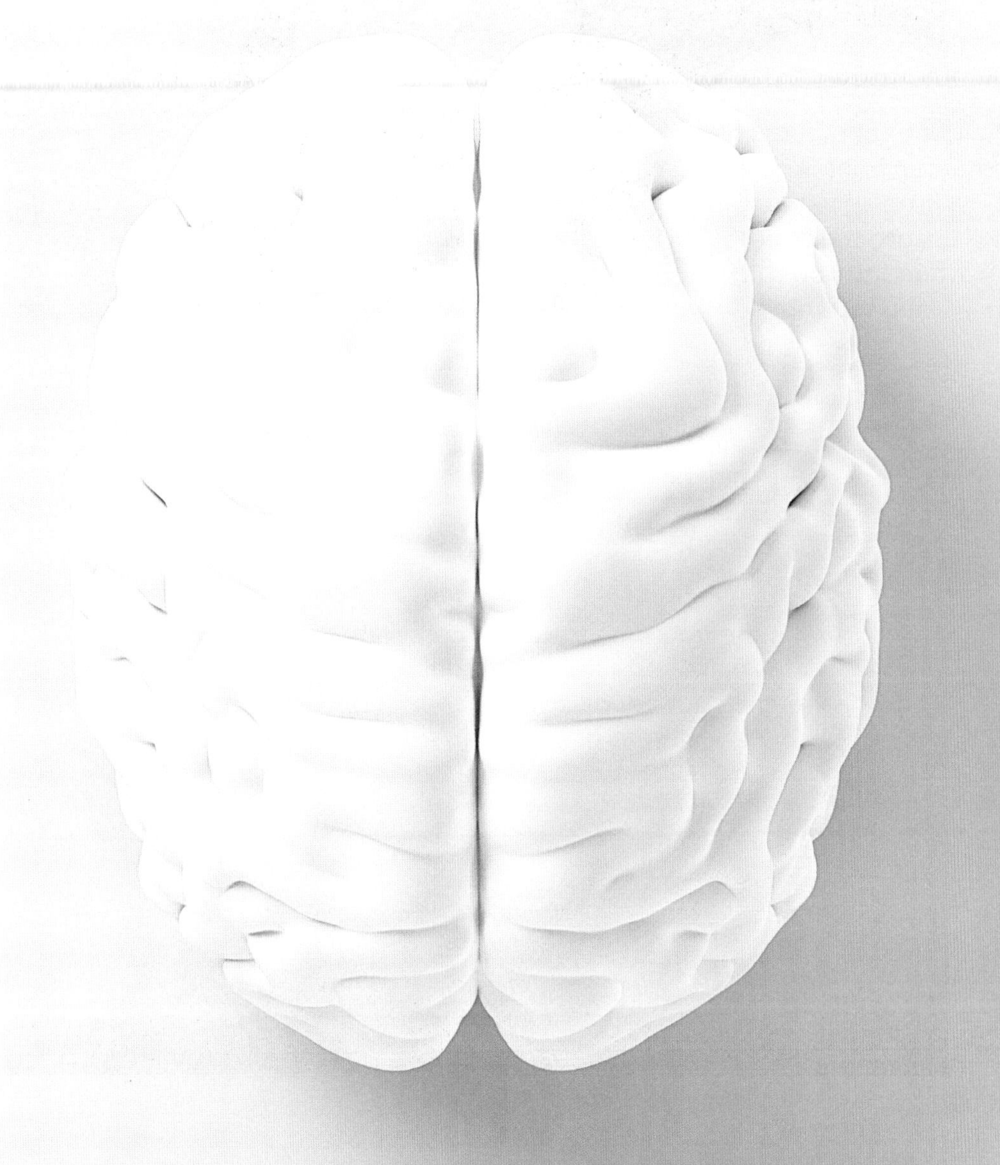

SHOCK ABSORBER

The underside of a horse's hoof is called a 'frog'. It helps to absorb the shock when the hoof hits the ground.

THE DEEP OCEAN

Ocean covers 70 per cent of the Earth's surface, but its depths remain almost completely unexplored. There are certain to be many amazing species that we have not yet discovered, some of which may only live at extreme depths or in unique environments.

NEVER-ENDING PATTERN

This amazing fractal image looks so innocent, but if you look at its centre and then slowly move the page closer and closer to your eyes you'll discover its more insidious side...

CAN YOU BELIEVE IT?

The image above contains a number of seemingly plausible – and yet impossible – connections between surfaces. And that's before you consider the fact that it's magically floating in mid-air...

TURNING TILES

The image above has a remarkable hypnotic effect. As you move your eyes around the image, look at each of the spiral centres in turn and you'll find that they start to turn – and at different rates, too!

DISAPPEARING ACT

Many creatures have evolved their own natural optical illusions to let them blend into their environments. The grey tree frog (*Hyla versicolor*) in this image provides perfect proof of that fact!

It blends in well with the trees, swamps and ponds that form its natural habitat.

NO BONES

Sharks have completely boneless skeletons, which instead consist purely of cartilage. They can also shed and replace as many as 35,000 teeth within their lifetime!

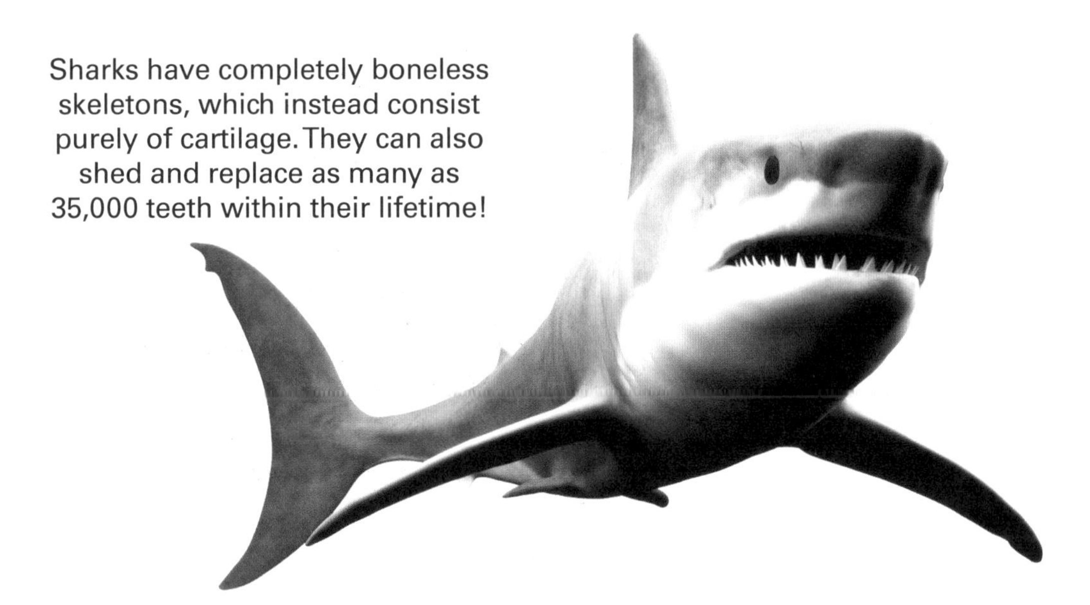

TURRET EYES

Chameleon eyes protrude from their head and are mounted on what are essentially tiny turrets. These turrets provide the ability to zoom in and out to identify food, in effect providing built-in telephoto lenses!

DOWN THE PLUGHOLE

It is often incorrectly claimed that water going down a plughole will rotate in different directions in the northern and southern hemispheres, thanks to the Coriolis effect. However this is too weak to have any significant effect in a household drain.

WHAT'S AROUND US?

The atmosphere of the Earth consists of 78 per cent nitrogen, and only 21 per cent of it is in fact oxygen.

DIRECT VIEW

No matter what angle you look at this picture from, the eyes will be looking straight back at you!

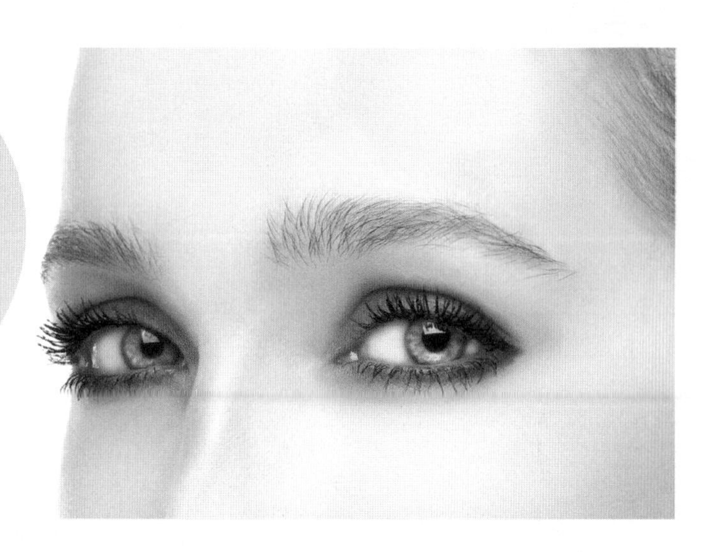

REAL SHAPE?

On first inspection this looks like a regular cylinder segment, or a washer – but on closer inspection the truth is revealed!

SOFT BUTTER

Spreadable butter can be manufactured by blending vegetable oil with regular butter, but another option is to simply feed the cows different food. If they are fed on a diet of rapeseed then the oil will naturally occur in their milk, producing a butter that can be spread straight from the fridge!

BIG JUMPERS

The red kangaroo can jump higher than any other animal. They've been recorded jumping up to 3.1 m (10 ft) into the air.

BACK AND FORTH

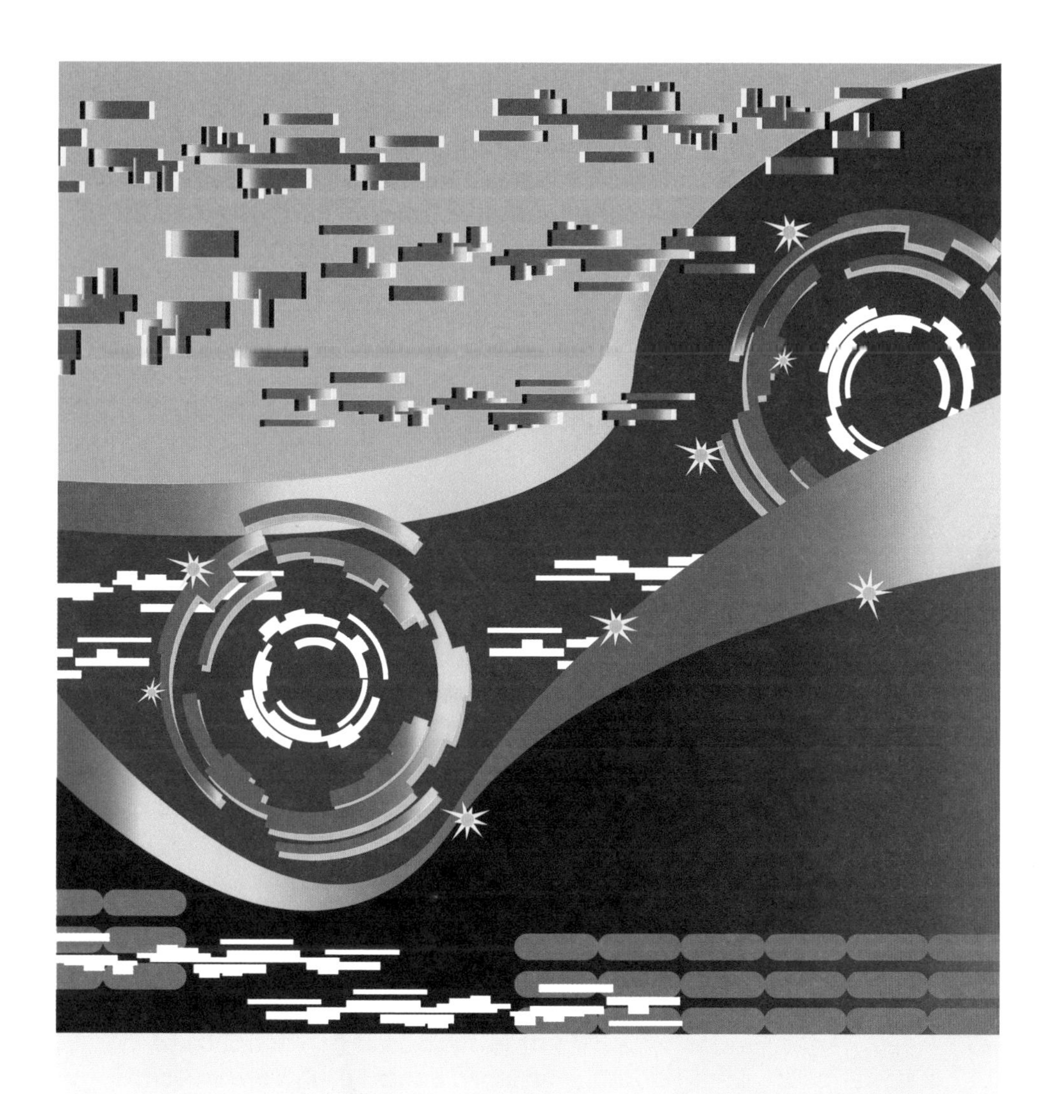

The rectangles at the top of this futuristic image appear to be moving back and forth in the air, like alien spaceships in an old computer game.

WORD RECORDS

The longest single-syllable English word is often claimed to be 'screeched', which is nine letters long. There is indeed no longer word in regular usage, but there are several other valid nine-letter single-syllable words, including 'scratched', 'scrounged', 'stretched' and 'strengths'! Meanwhile, the full Oxford English Dictionary also provides the ten-letter 'scraunched', which is an obsolete word meaning 'crunched noisily'.

The only English word starting and ending with a 'z' is 'zizz', referring to a buzzing sound.

WARPED CIRCLES

The rings in the shape below appear to be very uneven and far from circular – but each striped ring is in fact a perfect circle!

DEEP-SEA ACTIVITY

The giant squid is rarely seen alive and is mostly known only from bodies that have been found. Its maximum size is thought to be about 14 m (46 ft) long – that's almost as long as an articulated lorry. It also has the largest eyes of any animal, with one specimen measured at 27 cm (11 in) wide.

FREEZING POINT

Water ordinarily freezes at 0°C (32°F), but sea water freezes at -2°C (28.4°F) due to the large amount of salt present in it. As the sea freezes it pushes the salt out, so frozen sea water actually contains very little salt.

MAIN VEINS

The total length of veins in an adult human is about 60,000 miles (96,600 km) – that's almost two and a half times the circumference of the Earth, or 4.6 times the length of the Great Wall of China!

AMBIGRAM

nassau

The text above, 'nassau', is an example of an ambigram. In other words, it looks exactly the same when viewed upside down as when viewed right-side-up!

FIND THE CENTRE

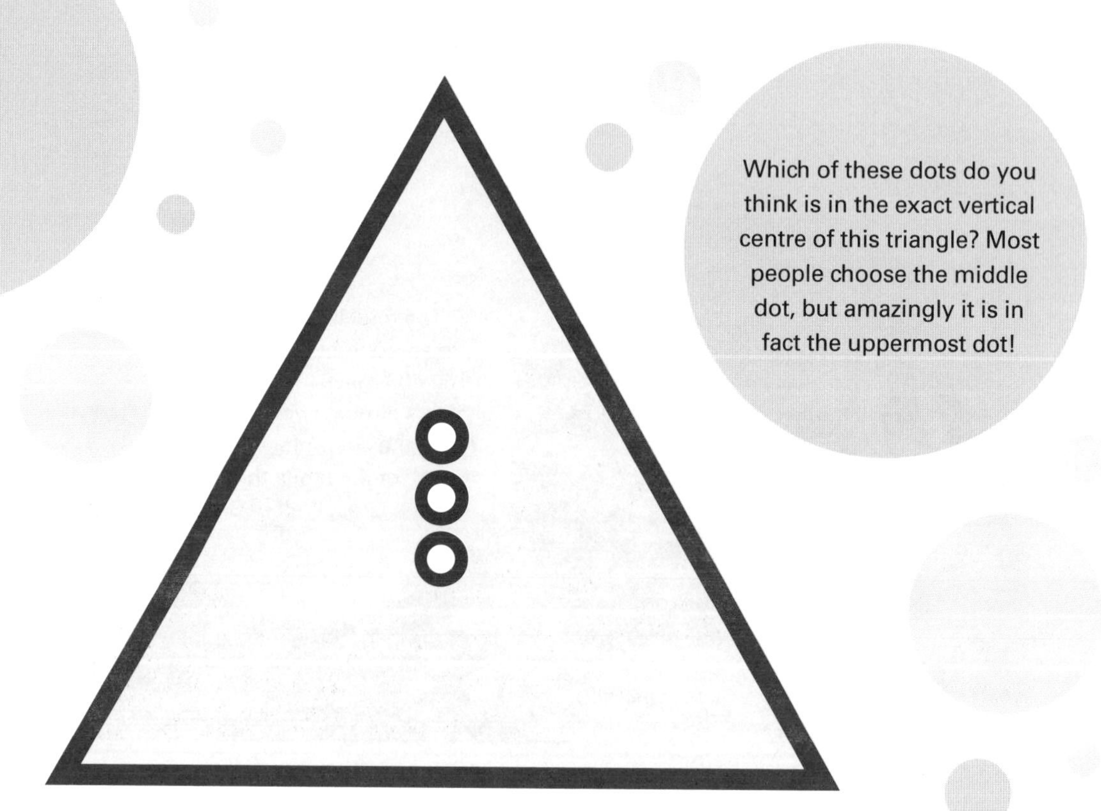

SEEING IS BELIEVING

Chameleons are the only animals that can move their eyes in two different directions at once. They also have monocular vision, so their brain can process the input from each eye completely separately from the other, which is a bit like watching two video screens at the same time! Other animals, such as prey animals like deer, have eyes that point in different directions, but they can't move them independently.

HUMAN GROWTH

Newborn babies have over 300 bones in their bodies, but these start to fuse together as they grow. By adulthood, there are only 206 separate bones in the human body.

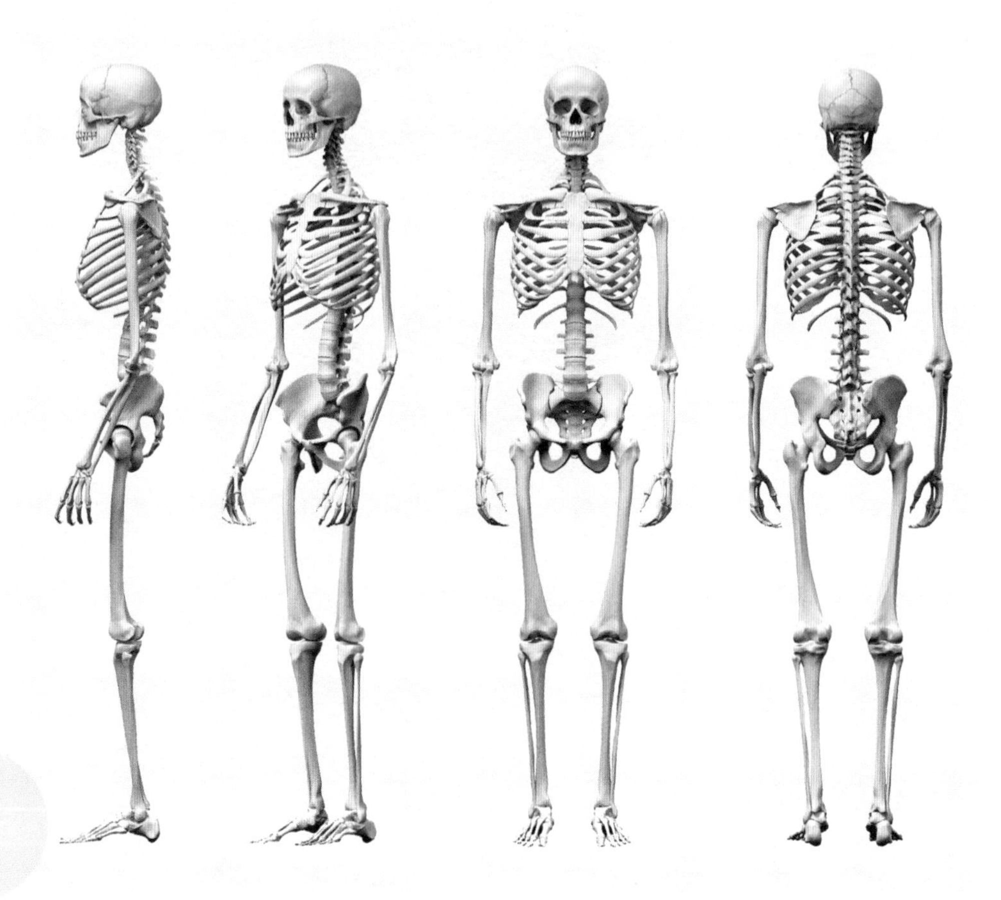

It was once believed, and is still thought to be the case by some, that both fingernails and hair would continue to grow for some time after death. This is not true, however.

GHOST DOTS

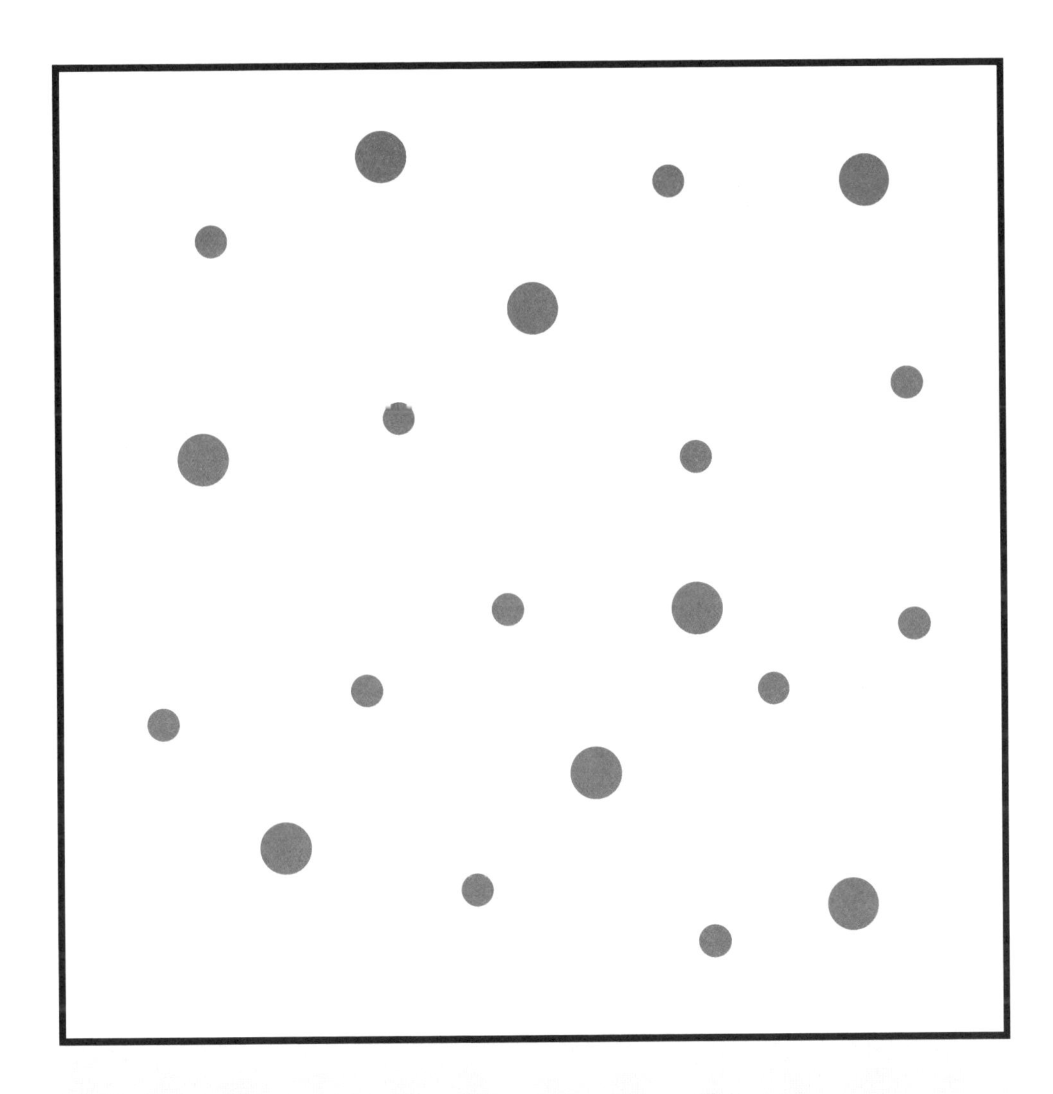

Look at any dot in the above picture for a second or two, then shift your gaze to another, and so on. You will see ghostly, super-bright dots floating in space as you move your eyes around. This is a persistence of vision effect.

TURNING FLOWERS

These circular patterns seem to come alive as you run your eyes over the picture. There is a really strong impression of circular movement.

JUST AN ILLUSION

In this pattern the blue and green lines appear to warp and bend as they travel across the image. In fact, all of the lines are perfectly straight. The horizontal and vertical lines, despite all being identical, are misleading your brain.

SLIDING BRICKS

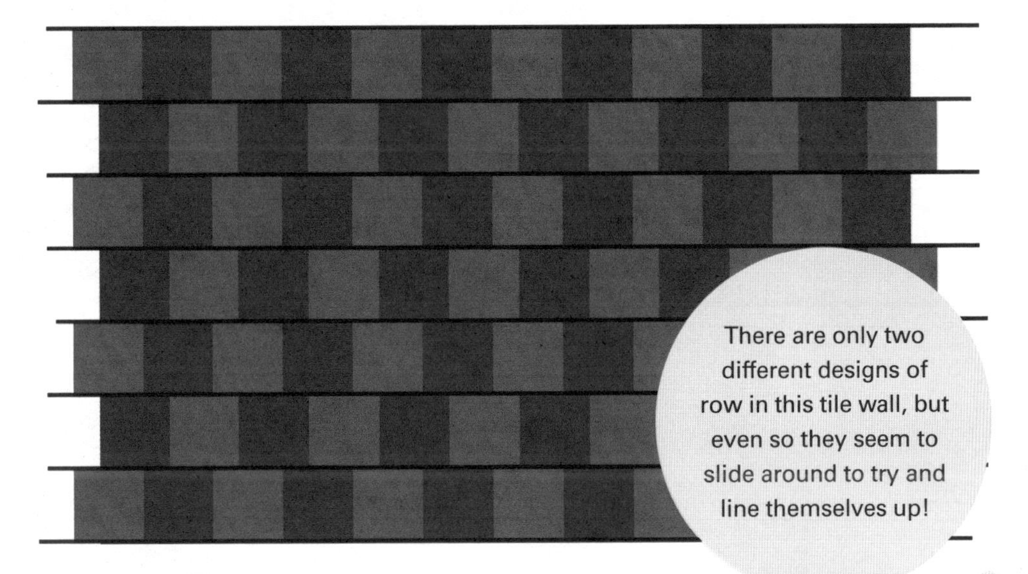

There are only two different designs of row in this tile wall, but even so they seem to slide around to try and line themselves up!

POLAR FUR

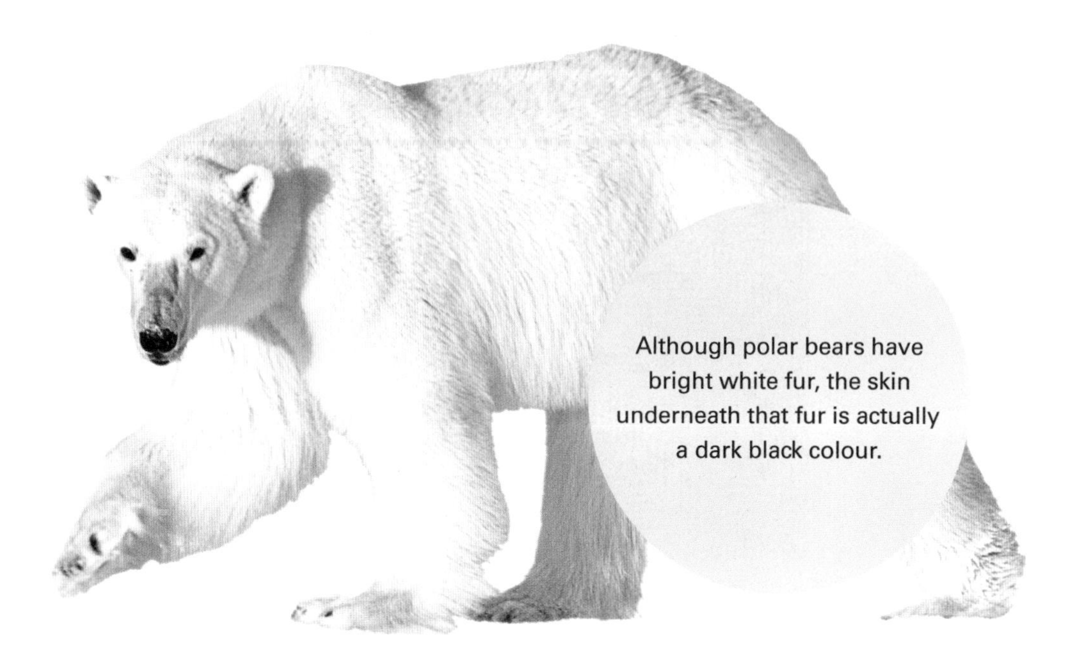

Although polar bears have bright white fur, the skin underneath that fur is actually a dark black colour.

EYE OF THE CAT

Cats are colour-blind, and are unable to tell red, green or brown apart from each other.

FIND TONGUE

Giraffe tongues are an amazing 45–50 cm (18–20 in) long, so that they can wrap them around tree branches and pull off the leaves. They're also a greyish purple colour, which is thought to stop the tongue from getting sunburnt when regularly exposed out on the savannah.

STARS IN YOUR EYES

If you're of a nervous disposition, look away now! This shimmering, vibrating, energetic, pulsing, shining pattern seems to be alive on the page.

GEOMETRY BUZZ

This geometric pattern consists of such strongly contrasting regions that it seems to buzz with an invisible energy. The effect gets even stronger if you let your eyes go slightly out of focus while looking at it.

FOLLOW YOUR NOSE

The proboscis monkey is well named, since its nose is so large that it can't eat unless it pushes its nose out of the way first! When threatened, its nose gets even larger, making its voice louder so it can warn others of impending danger.

LOOK UP AND DOWN

Run your eyes in a vertical direction up and down this pattern, and you will see bands of different shades of green shift and move within the image as you do.

UP, UP AND AWAY

Modern balloons are made of latex, or, if it is a foil balloon, from aluminium-coated nylon. Earlier balloons, however, were made from animal bladders – pig bladders were particularly popular! Great fun to blow up with your mouth!

LEGO® LEGIONS

The world's largest population group is... LEGO® minifigures! Over 5 billion have been produced since they were first made in 1978. Until 2003, however, all LEGO® minifigures had bright yellow faces.

ON THE NOSE

Dogs have extremely sensitive noses, which are powerful enough to detect the smell of lung cancer in humans. They can even sniff out the scent of the disease long before symptoms develop. Dogs have also been shown to be able to smell early stage breast cancer and skin cancer.

MAGIC WATERWHEEL

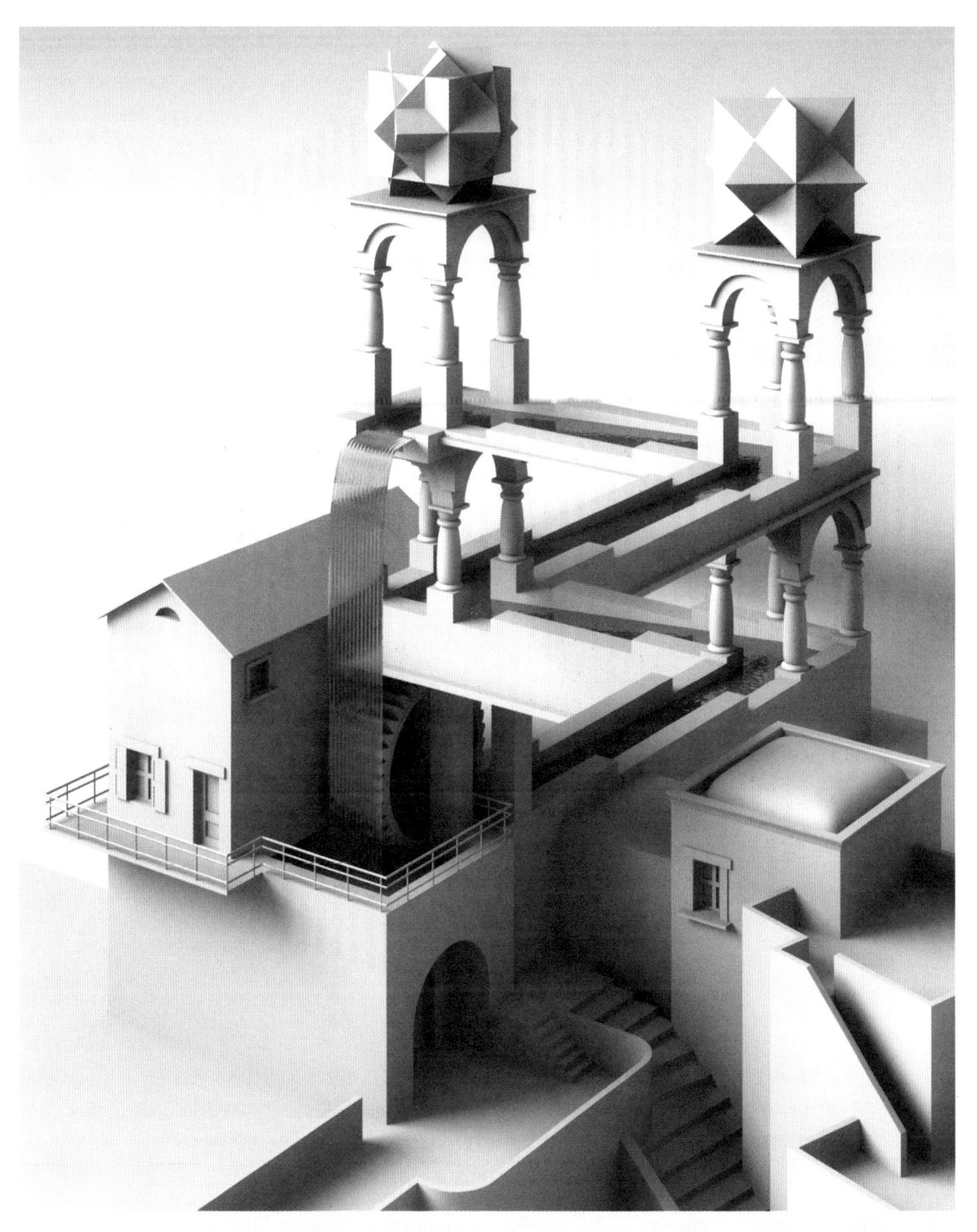

This perpetual-motion waterwheel system would solve the world's energy needs if only it could be built in reality! This image is a modern computer-generated recreation of Escher's classic 1961 *Waterfall* image.

HOW MANY ORANGES?

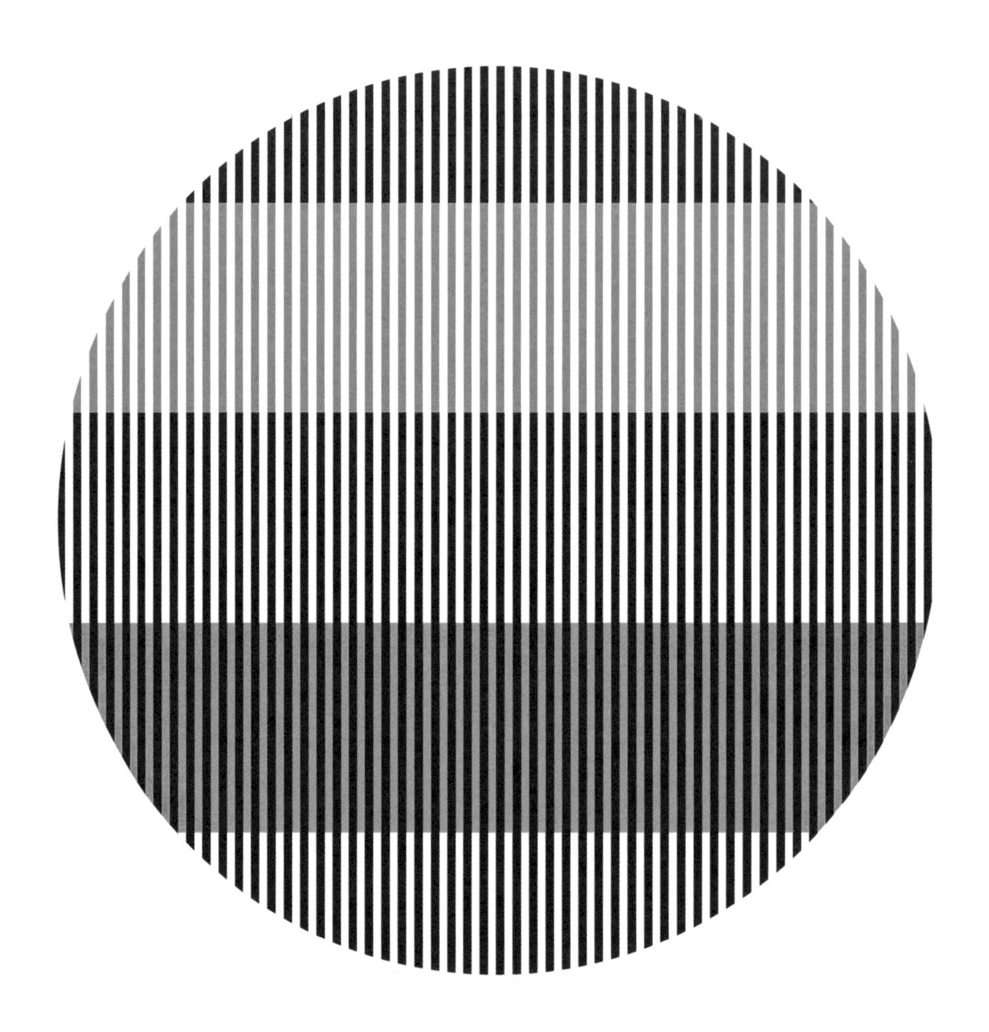

How many shades of orange do you see in the image above? In fact there is only one – the overlapping black and white lines contrast so strongly that they affect your perception of the orange.

WATER WRINKLES

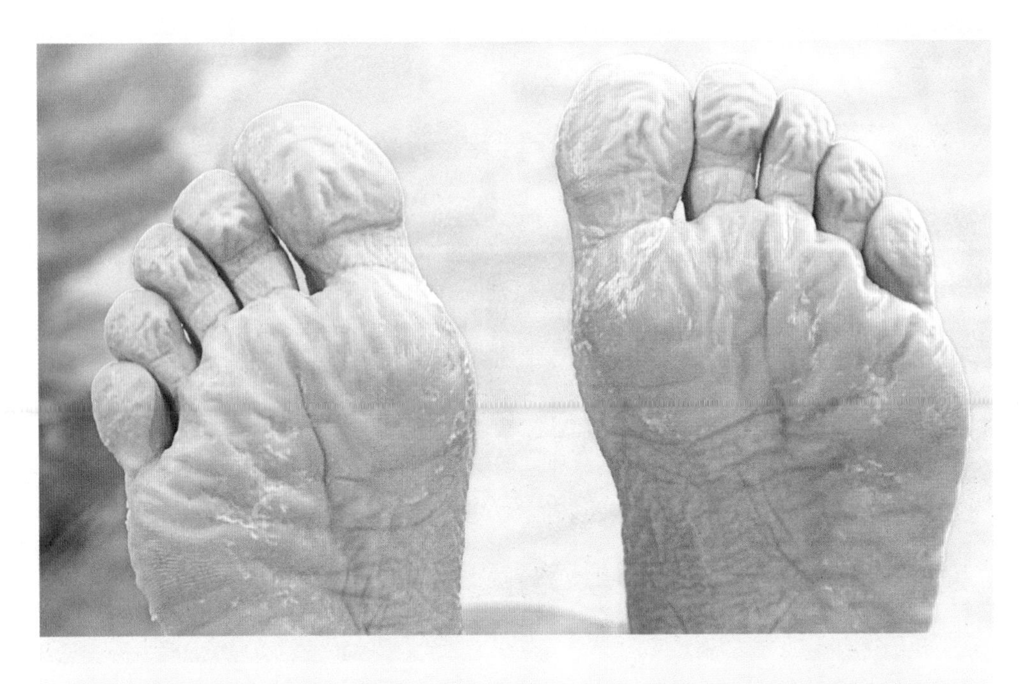

When skin is exposed to water for prolonged periods of time it becomes wrinkled. This is not due to it absorbing water, but due to a nervous system response which may have evolved to give a better grip in wet environments.

DAILY ROUTINE

An average person will use the bathroom approximately six times each day.

WHALE CONTROL

Trinity Church in New York City, at the junction of Wall Street and Broadway, has a royal charter dating from 1697 that gives it control over any whales washing up on the banks of the city. The church still maintains this claim.

NO REPEATS

The longest English word that doesn't repeat any letters is 'uncopyrightable'. However, there is a second, much rarer, alternative word too in the form of 'dermatoglyphics', which is the study of skin patterning.

SPINNING WHEEL

This fairground wheel seems to spin all by itself, thanks to the lighting highlights on each of the cars.

LENGTH TO LENGTH

Which of these two arrows is longer? Most people would choose the line on the left, but in fact both are exactly the same length! The yellow shape creates a false perspective.

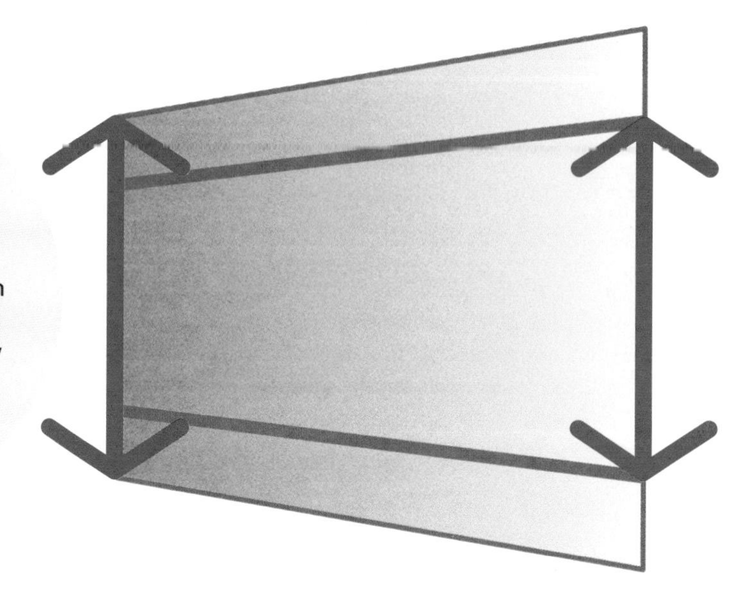

WHAT DO YOU SEE?

At first glance this seems to be a picture of a woman, but look a little closer and you'll see that it is also two crows sitting on a waiter-like mannequin.

WATER, WATER

There is more fresh water in the atmosphere than in all of the rivers on the planet combined.

HAMSTER FACTS

Hamsters have a shorter pregnancy period than any other placental mammal – just 16 days! Each litter can contain 20 or more young, and the mother can become pregnant again immediately.

Amazingly, all pet golden hamsters are descended from a single brother and sister pairing made in the 1930s. Prior to that, researchers had been unable to breed and domesticate hamsters.

IMPOSSIBLE DOMINOES

This game of impossible dominoes would be rather hard to play in reality, but you could certainly have fun trying!

WORLD NUMBERS

There are over 7 billion people alive on Earth right now, out of around 110 billion who have ever lived. If everyone alive right now stood right next to one another, they'd fit into an area of 500 square miles (1,300 square km).

CLOSE CAPITALS

The capital of Western Australia, Perth, is closer to the capital of Indonesia, Jakarta, than it is to Australia's own capital, Canberra.

MARINE VISION

All marine mammals have monochromatic vision, meaning that they can only see in black and white. This is likely to have evolved because most colour information is lost once you travel a short distance beneath the surface of the ocean, so there is no need for this ability.

DISNEY'S ROOTS

Walt Disney's unusual surname was due to his French ancestry. His ancestor Robert d'Isigny, from the French town of Isigny-sur-Mer, settled in England after the Norman Conquest in 1066. The family later anglicized the name as 'Disney', keeping the pronunciation but in the process disguising their French roots.

UNDULATING SHAPES

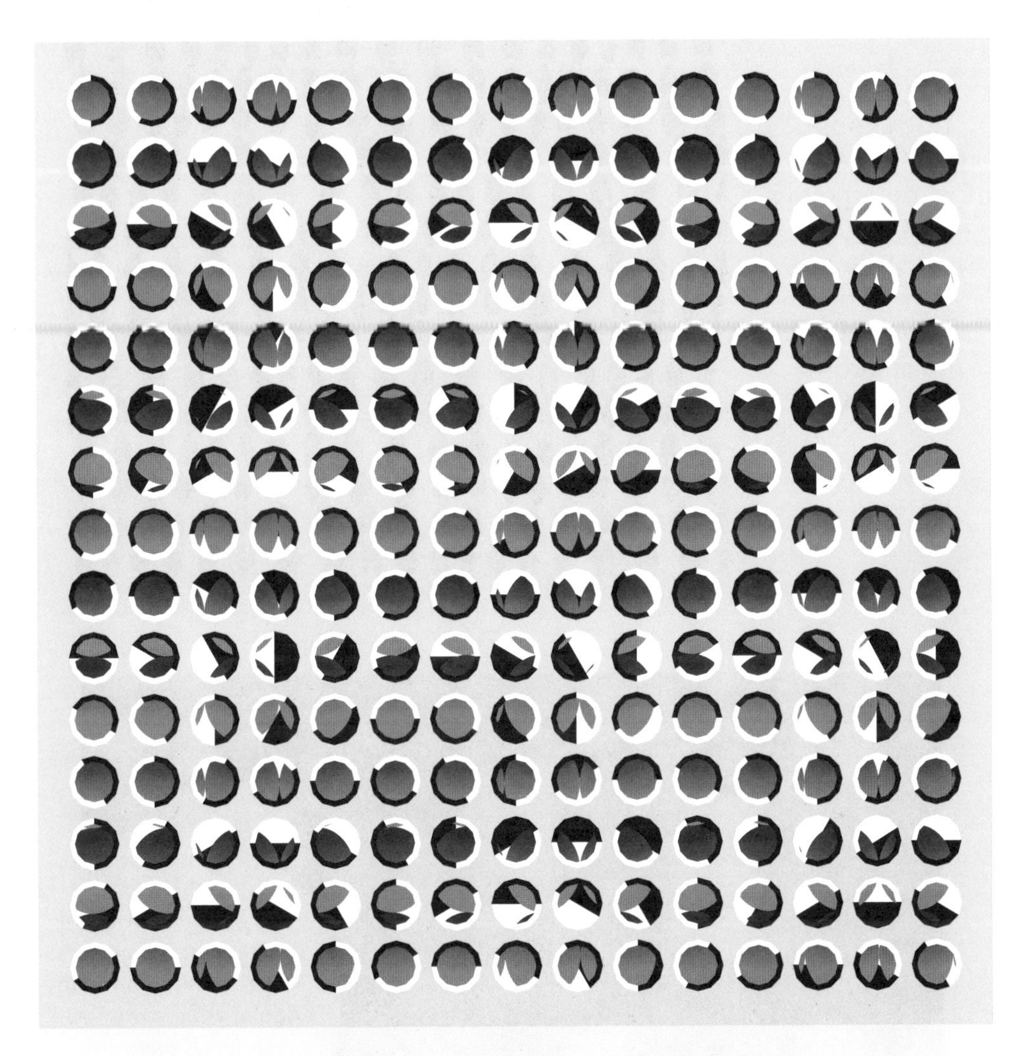

It's hard to tell what lies underneath these circles, but as you try and work it out so the image will ripple and move in a most disconcerting way!

SWAYING AND SLIDING

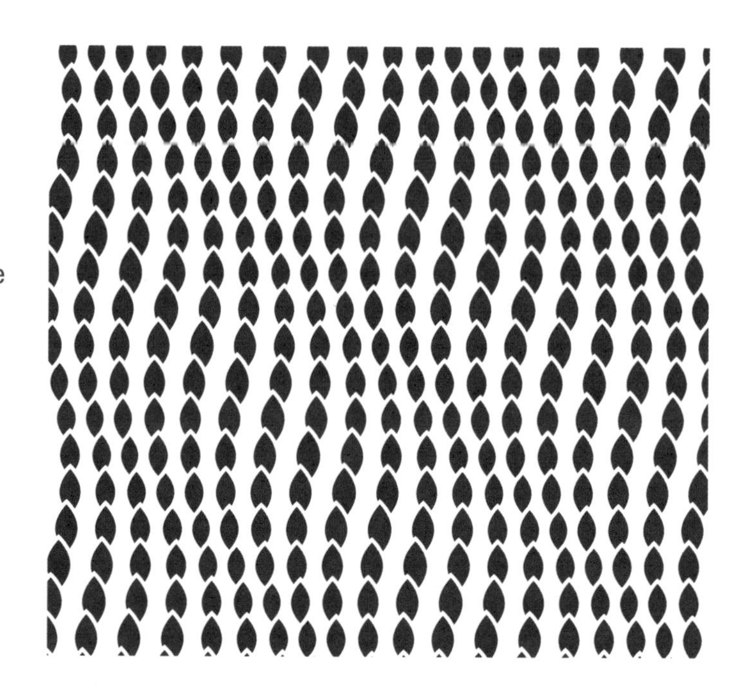

This simple pattern has a most remarkable effect on your brain. Without even any shading cues, the columns seem to sway.

If you look at this text and try to see the image behind out of the edge of your vision, you'll see the shapes start to slide around...

THE NATURE OF NUTS

Peanuts are neither nuts nor indeed peas, but are actually a type of legume.

NO RHYME

No English word fully rhymes with 'orange', although there are half-rhymes such as 'lozenge' – half-rhymes are so-called because the vowels are not the same. By the same token there is also no word that fully rhymes with 'silver'.

MMM AND MMM...

M&M's® chocolates are named after Forrest Mars, the son of the founder of the Mars® chocolate company, and Bruce Murrie, the son of the founder of the Hershey® chocolate company. That's why there's an apostrophe in the name. They were introduced in 1940, with the peanut variety following in 1954.

LENGTHY BILL

The only bird to have a beak that's longer than its body is the sword-billed hummingbird. Its beak is so long, at 7–10 cm (3–4 in), that it's bigger than the entire body of some other hummingbirds!

SUPER-LONG NAME

The longest single-word place name in a country with English as its national language is

Taumatawhakatangihangakoau-auotamateaturipukakapikimaunga-horonukupokaiwhenuakitanatahu

on the North Island of New Zealand. It means 'The summit where Tamatea, the man with the big knees, the climber of mountains, the land-swallower who travelled about, played his nose flute to his loved one'.

BRASS CUBES

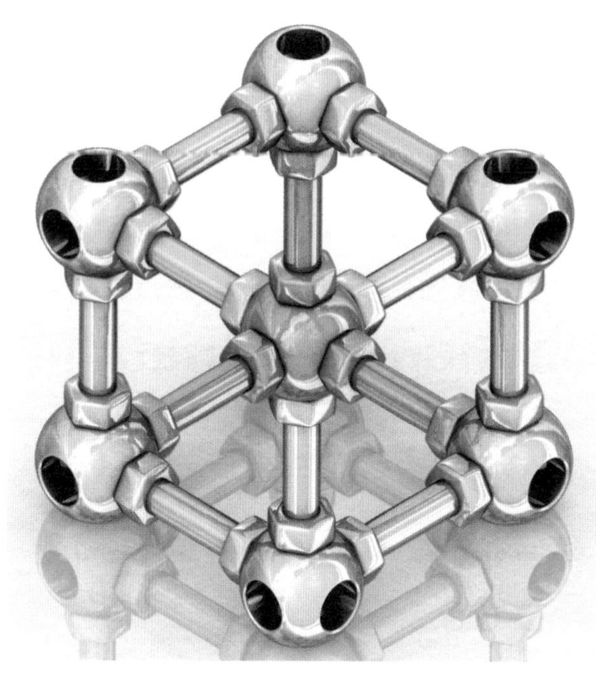

This brass shape looks rather solid, but if you tried constructing it you'd find it's anything but! The centre shape is somehow both at the back and at the front, if you look at its connections.

POINT THE ARROW

This arrow points in two directions, that's for sure. Deciding which two directions it actually points in, however, is much more difficult to discern!

WATER RUNNER

Basilisk lizards have the unique ability to run on water, thanks to flaps between their toes. They can run for about 4.5 m (15 ft) before they start to slow down and sink, or if they choose to walk on all fours then they can travel for closer to 6 m (20 ft).

CONSTANT ORBIT

The yin-yang symbols appear to orbit the centre of the image in a most peaceful way...

LABOUR OF LOVE

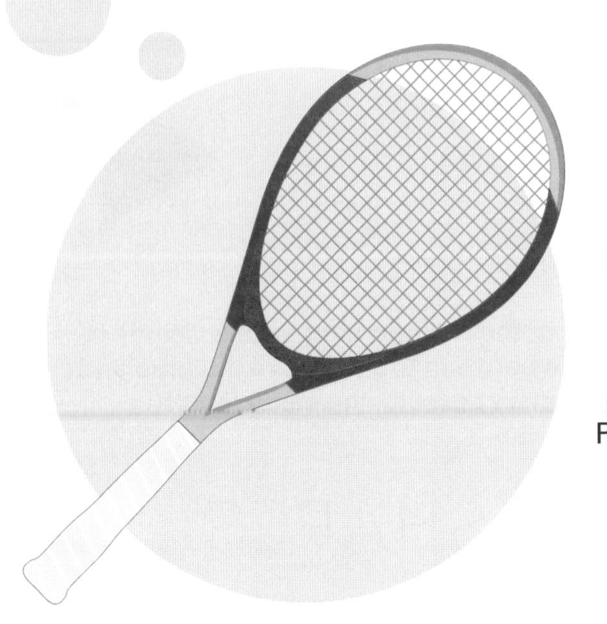

In tennis, 'love' means no score – the term may derive from the phrase 'play for love', or in other words for the love of the game and not for anything else. Players with no points don't have anything, so they have 'love'.

ANY NEWS?

On Good Friday, 1930, the BBC (British Broadcasting Corporation) replaced a new bulletin with an announcement that 'There is no news'. They then played some jolly piano music to fill the dead air.

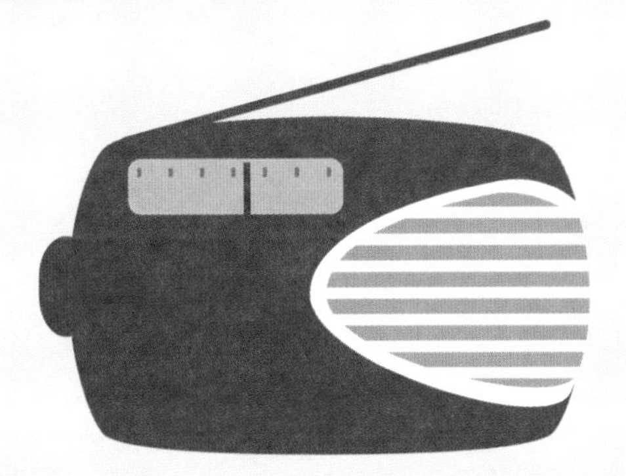

RELATIVE DISTANCE

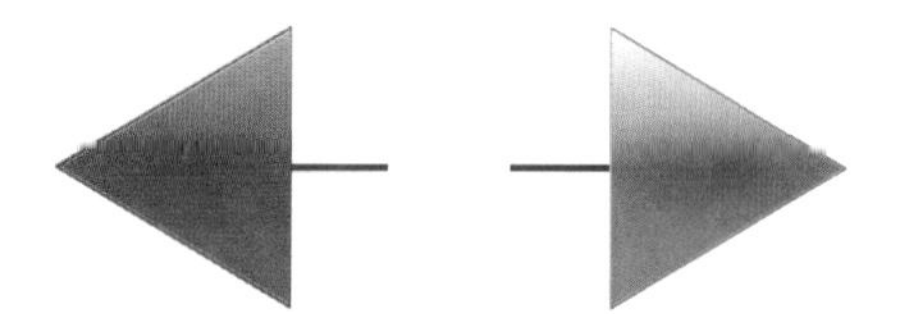

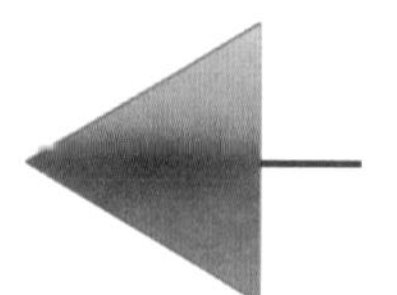

The distance between the points of the red and blue arrows seems to be much shorter than the distance between the points of the blue and green arrows – but they are in fact exactly the same length!

FLOATING SHAPES

This perspective drawing, made outside a Dutch office building, wappears to show some abstract shapes floating above a garden oasis.

ENDLESS ROLLS

The residents of the USA use enough toilet paper each year to stretch all the way to the Sun – and back!

MISQUOTE

Marie Antoinette never actually said 'Let them eat cake,' when responding to reports of people without any food. The quote is in fact derived from a book written in 1767, when Marie Antoinette was only 12 years old.

ANIMAL FACTS

The hyrax, named from the Greek for 'shrewmouse', indeed looks just like a rodent but is in fact closely related to the elephant! Their biological similarities include tusks which develop from their incisor teeth, like elephants, whereas most mammals develop tusks from their canines.

VISION WHIRL

If you fix your eyes on the black dot in the centre of this image and then move your head – or the book – slowly closer to the picture, you should see the outer parts of the pattern start to spin.

HEAVY WEIGHT

William Howard Taft has the unique distinction of having been the heaviest President of the USA. He weighed over 160 kg (350 lb), and the chief White House usher at the time claimed he once got stuck in the White House bath! After he ceased to be president, however, he lost 32 kg (70 lb) within a year.

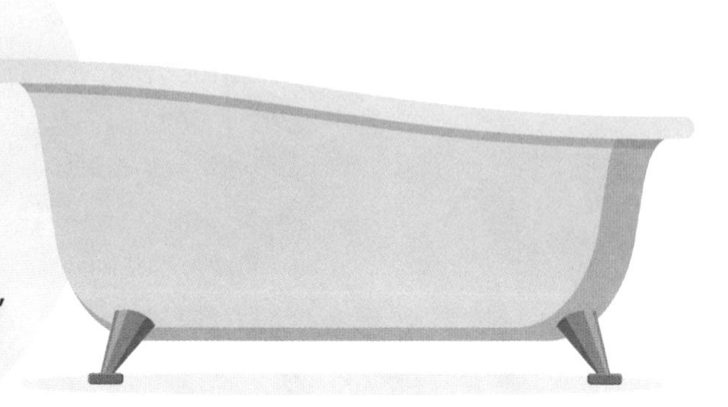

CLOSE GOODBYE

The second and third presidents of the USA, John Adams and Thomas Jefferson, both died independently on the same day within hours of each other, on 4 July 1826.

SKEWED LINES

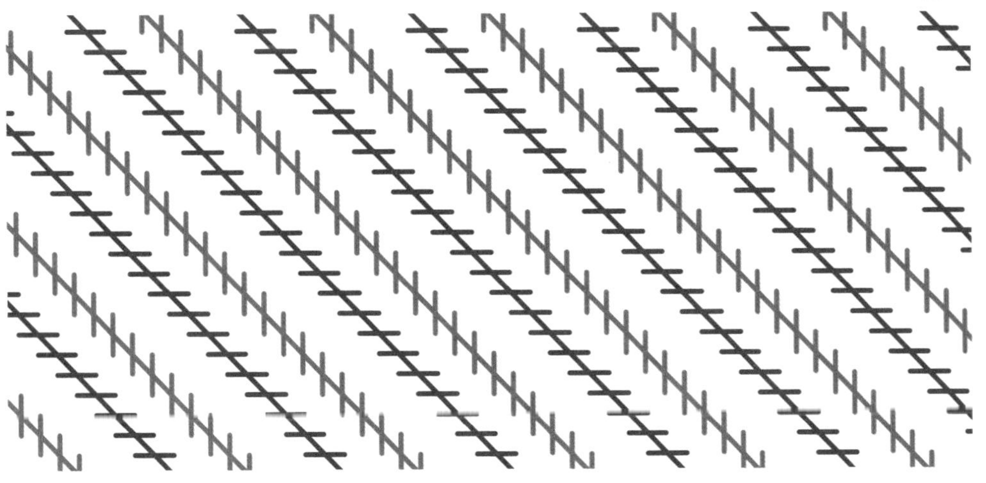

This effect is called the Zöllner Illusion, after the German astrophysicist who first discovered that drawing cross-hatch marks on parallel lines makes them appear to bend – these lines are in fact all perfectly parallel!

STAR SHINE

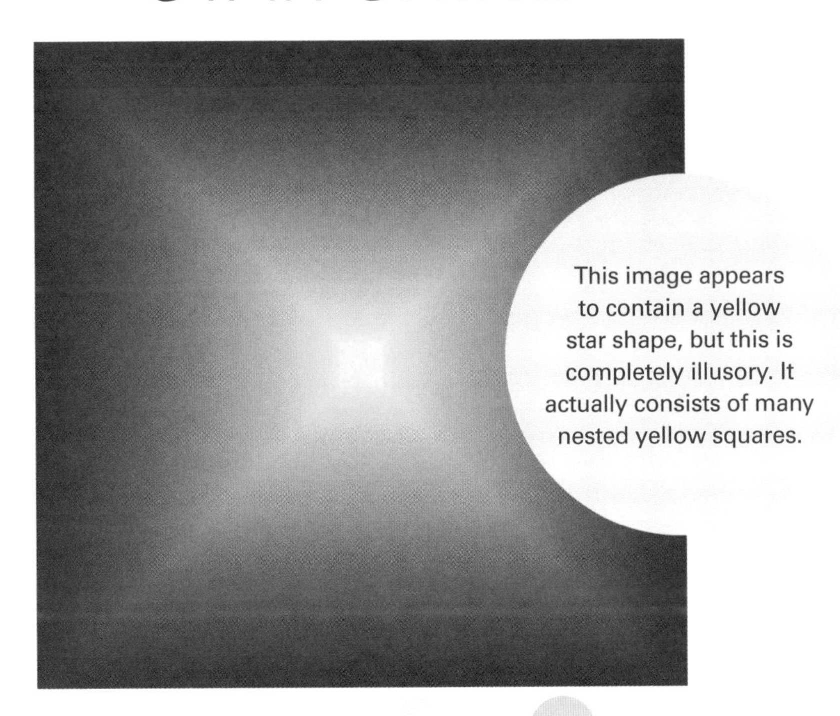

This image appears to contain a yellow star shape, but this is completely illusory. It actually consists of many nested yellow squares.

NOT POSSIBLE!

This classical edifice could be a remnant of the Ancient Greeks... or at least it could have been, were it not impossible to build! The top of the shape is straight, but the column bases don't match up with this alignment.

DISTORTED PATHS

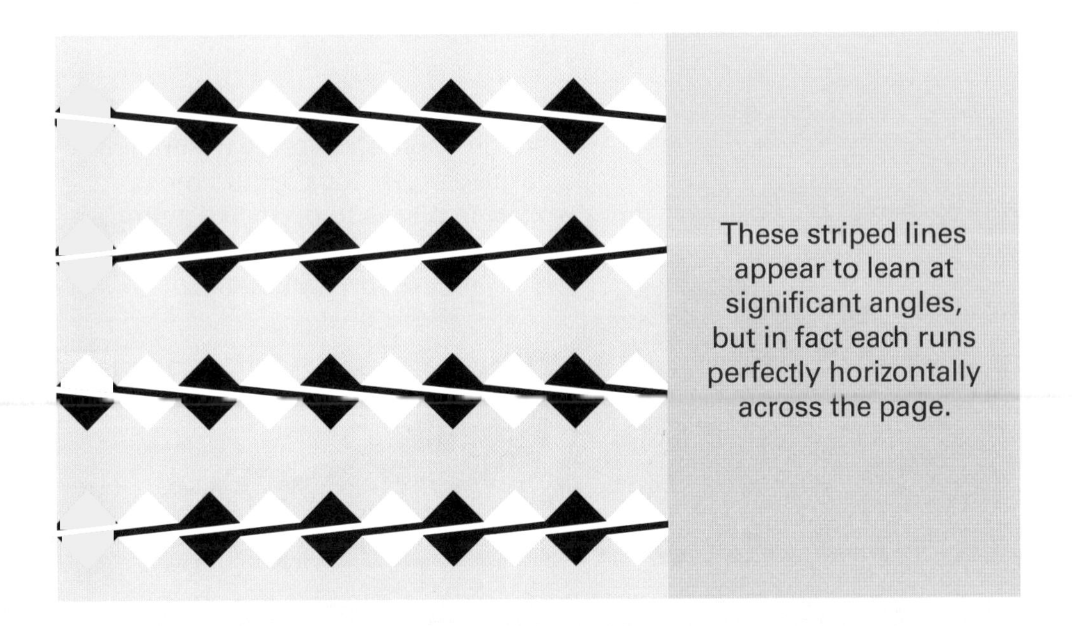

These striped lines appear to lean at significant angles, but in fact each runs perfectly horizontally across the page.

GLOWING SQUARES

The paper in the centre of these shapes seems to glow whiter-than-white, and even slightly brown on the right. Try covering over the surrounding area, however, and this will be revealed as an illusion.

IRON FEATS

In the sport of Extreme Ironlng, thrill-seekers look for the most extreme places to do their ironing, such as while bungee jumping or high-up on mountains.

HIGH-SCORING GAME

The record for the largest Rugby World Cup win is a whopping 142–0! This feat was achieved by Australia in 2003, when they defeated Namibia. The most points in a single game were achieved by New Zealand in 1995, when they beat Japan 145–17.

SNEEZE SPEED

It's frequently claimed that a human sneeze can leave the body at over 100 mph (160 km/h). The reality is much slower, although still impressive, being closer to 40 mph (65 km/h).

UNIQUE PRINTS

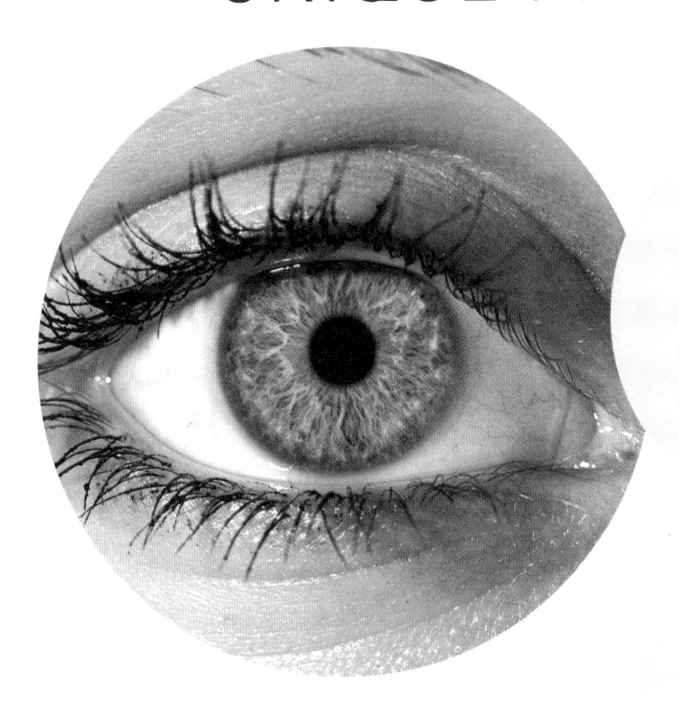

As well as unique fingerprints, every person also has a unique tongue print and iris pattern.

SWIMMING FISH

The fish in this tank seem to swim back and forth as you look around the tank. The illusion is created by the striped pattern on each fish.

IN THE WINGS

You wouldn't easily spot this camouflaged butterfly unless you really knew what you were looking for! Only its shadow gives it away.

FISH FACTS

A blue whale's tongue weighs around 2,700 kg (6,000 lb), and its mouth is large enough to hold 90,000 kg (14,173 stone) of food and water. Despite this, its throat is so relatively narrow that it cannot swallow any object wider than a beach ball.

The dogfish is, somewhat ironically, actually a species of cat shark!

GRADUATED SHADES

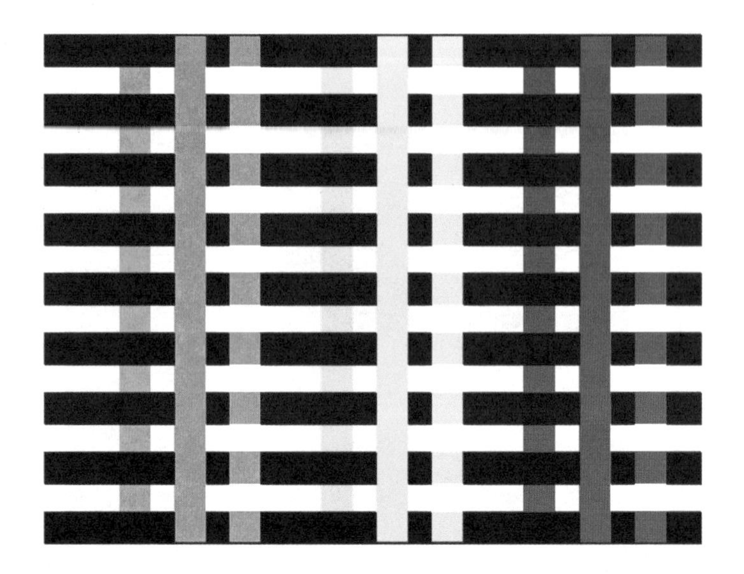

There seem to be three shades of each of these vertical strips. In reality, however, each group of three uses only a single colour. The effect is caused by the interleaved white and black bars.

LOOK CENTRE

What colour is the central shape in the image? If you think it's green, then think again! It's actually a perfect grey. The surrounding purple hue misleads the eye.

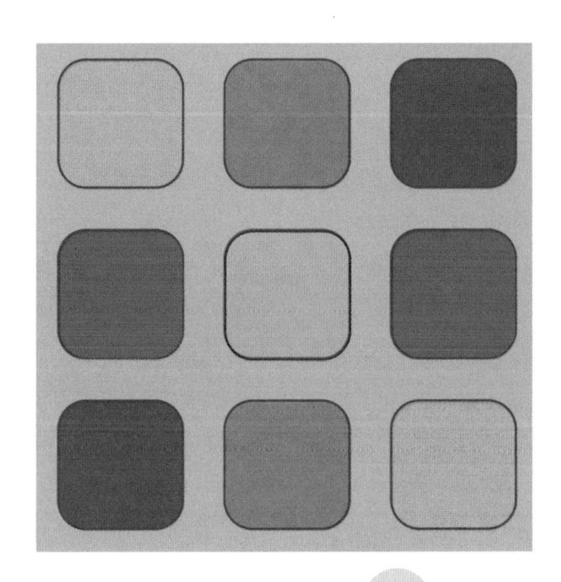

DNA BREAKTHROUGH

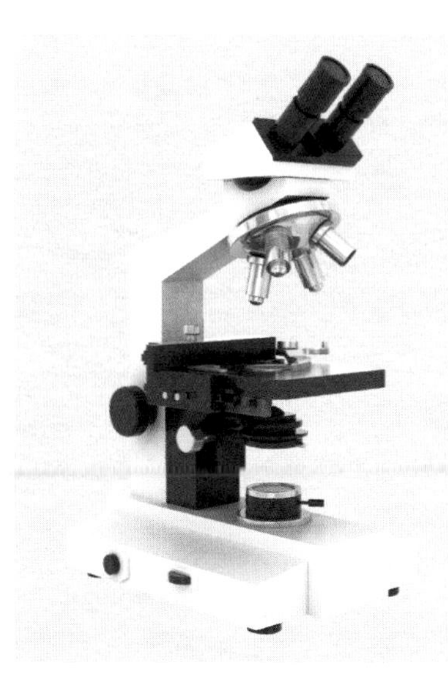

When the discovery of the structure of DNA, the fundamental building block of life, was first publicly announced in 1953, the *New York Times* reported it briefly in an early edition but considered it so unimportant that the story was replaced in later editions.

FUN AND GAMES

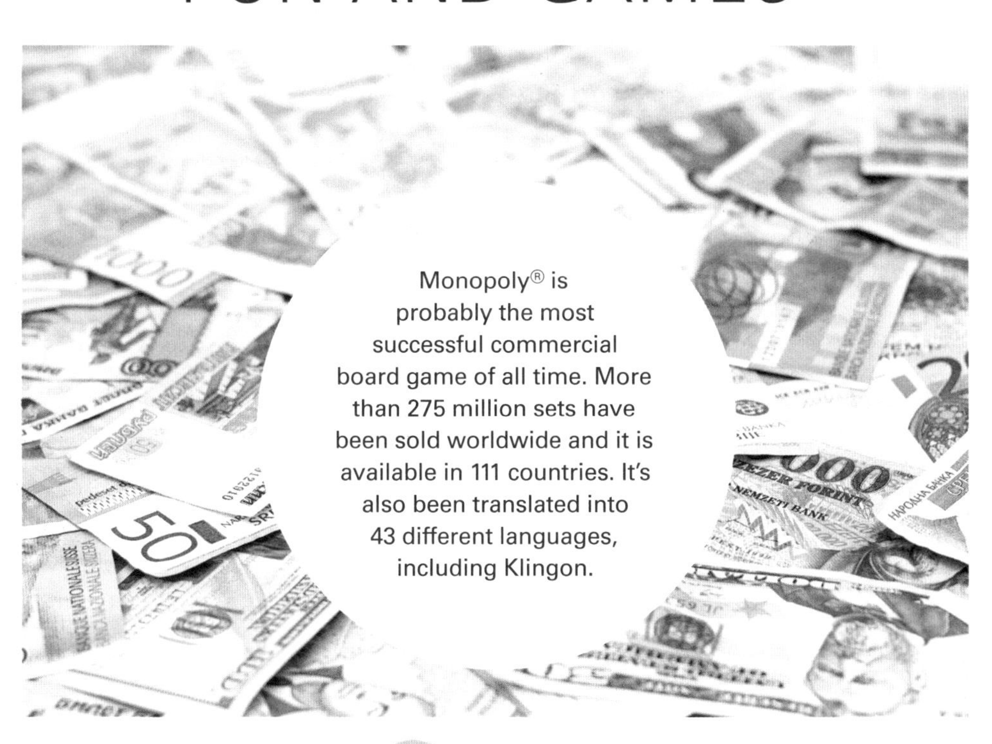

Monopoly® is probably the most successful commercial board game of all time. More than 275 million sets have been sold worldwide and it is available in 111 countries. It's also been translated into 43 different languages, including Klingon.

ANIMAL MAGIC

FULL OF GOOD BOOKS

The third President of the USA, Thomas Jefferson, collected so many books over his lifetime that in 1814 he single-handedly restocked the USA's Library of Congress with 6,487 of his own books. The original collection had been lost when the British set it on fire! His donation more than doubled the number of books the library had held prior to the fire.

TURNING MOSAIC

This wheel mosaic doesn't need a motor to start turning – just looking at it will entirely suffice!

DOVE OR ANGEL?

At first sight this looks like a picture of a dove flying through the air. But look a bit closer and you'll see that it's also an angel in flight.

DOUBLE TAKE

Is this a beautifully sculpted column, or is it the silhouette of two people facing one another?

PARLIAMENT RULES

If you died in the UK Houses of Parliament, you would come under the jurisdiction of the royal household's coroner since officially it remains a royal palace. It is often claimed this also entitles you to a state funeral, but unsurprisingly this is not true and has never been the case. It is, however, illegal to enter the Houses of Parliament while wearing a suit of armour.

FLOATING ON AIR

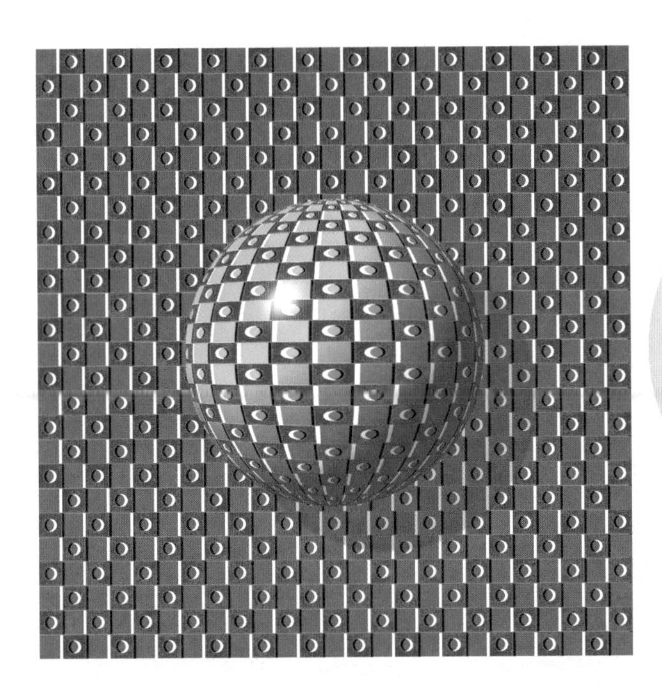

This sphere appears to be floating in front of the page, while the background of the picture seems to be slowly floating past.

GET THE BLUES

It might be hard to believe, but the shade of blue marked with the arrow at the top is identical to the shade of blue marked with the lower arrow!

DISTANT BUILDING

The main part of this building seems to be very distant from the viewer, given the difficulty in making out the stairs in the distance – but if you look closely at the nearest steps you'll see that it's an architectural illusion.The staircase features very shallow steps to create the illusion of a much larger building.

FISHY BUSINESS

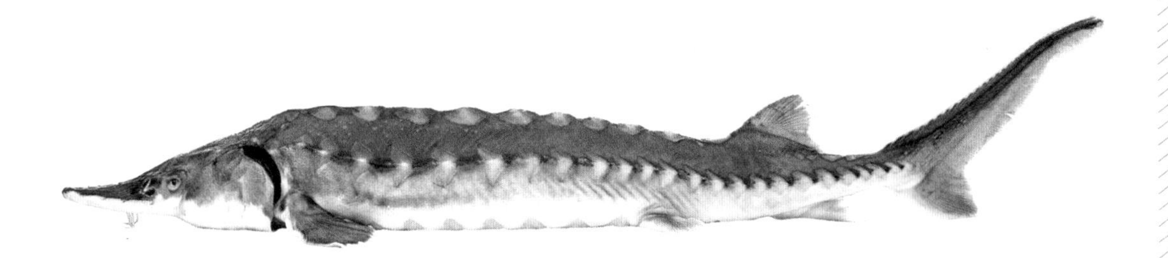

Thanks to a Royal Prerogative from 1324, any whale or sturgeon found on the British coast belongs to the monarch. Even if the monarch gives permission to keep it, it is still illegal to sell it.

VOTING REGS

In Australia, it is illegal not to vote in a federal election or referendum. If those eligible to vote cannot give an acceptable reason for failing to vote, they can be sent to court. The court can then issue a fine and record a criminal conviction against them.

UNSETTLED STRIPS

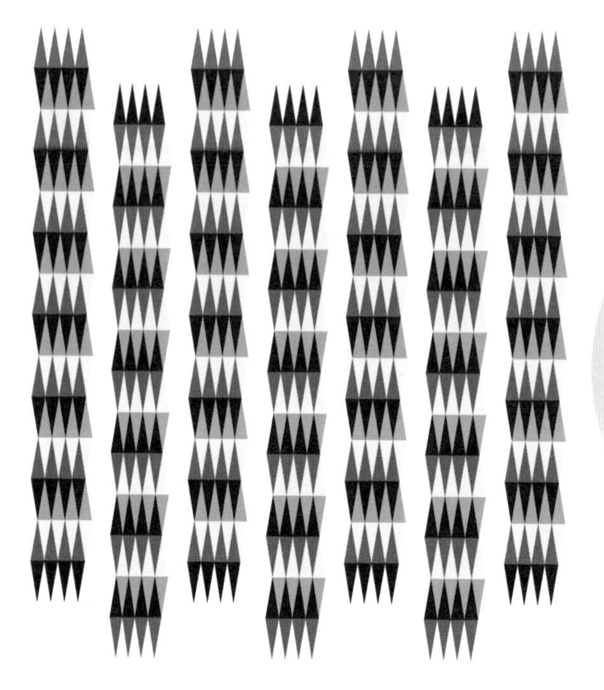

These strips are made up of a relatively simple diamond pattern, but however you look at them they appear to be sliding up and down the page!

UP AND ACROSS

In this simple image, does the area around the horizontal stripes appear to be a different shade or colour to that around the vertical stripes? The vertical sections look much brighter than the horizontal sections.

TENNIS RECORD

Rafael Nadal has won more gentlemans' singles titles at any one given Grand Slam tennis tournament than any other player in history. He took this record in 2013, when he won the French Open for an incredible eighth time. Having won it again since, his record looks virtually unassailable.

MULTI-COLOURED VEG

Carrots can be grown in a range of colours, including purple, yellow, red, white and – of course – orange. Surprisingly, the ubiquitous modern orange carrot was not widely grown until the 17th century.

FLAMINGO DISH

Flamingo's tongue was quite the delicacy in Ancient Rome, where it was served in a delightful dish that also included pheasant brains and parrotfish livers. Also particularly popular were fattened dormice, and hosts would sometimes have them weighed in front of their guests as a show of their wealth and status.

LOVING LANGUAGE

The longest regular English word that was not deliberately created just to be long, or is of purely technical meaning, is antidisestablishmentarianism – it means 'opposition to the disestablishment of the Church of England'.

The UK's Poet Laureate is traditionally rewarded each year with a butt of canary (a sweet sherry) or sack (a dry sherry). This is equivalent to around 650 bottles, although cash payments are sometimes accepted in lieu of all this alcohol.

PULSATING WINGS

This pattern, constructed from four butterfly shapes, appears to shrink inwards into the centre of each butterfly, even as you read this text. Try looking at the centre of one butterfly and then, when the image stops moving, shift your gaze to the centre of another butterfly, and so on.

SPINNING DISCS

The picture above consists of an arrangement of spinning discs. As you look around the image you should see the discs that you aren't directly looking at spinning. This effect is caused by the white highlights.

PAN FOREVER

Several of the songs that appear on Meat Loaf's Bat Out of Hell album were originally written for a musical version of *Peter Pan*.

In the UK, *Peter Pan* has a special copyright status. It has been protected in perpetuity by Act of Parliament so that its copyright never expires. This means that Great Ormond Street Hospital, to whom its author J. M. Barrie gave the rights, can continue to receive money from *Peter Pan* for evermore.

BRICK-TASTIC FACT

If it were possible to build a column of 40 billion standard-height LEGO® bricks, you'd be able to touch the Moon!

LOSING AIR

This ball provides the rather strong impression that it is slowly deflating into its centre!

KEEP TO A RHYME

Research has found that people are more likely to believe a statement if it rhymes than if it does not. Rhyming statements also tend to be more memorable.

PLANET NAMES

Until the late 1990s it was agreed that there were nine planets in our solar system. Astronomers then started to dispute whether Pluto was a planet or not. The International Astronomical Union decided in 2006 to call Pluto a dwarf planet, making the number of 'real' planets in our solar system eight.

HELIUM FACT

The chemical element with the lowest melting point is Helium, at -272°C (-457.6°F). This means that it will not freeze at normal atmospheric pressure under any circumstance.

BUILD UP

The original Elizabethan Globe Theatre in London was deliberately built in a similar style to the Roman Colosseum.

DANCING PATTERNS

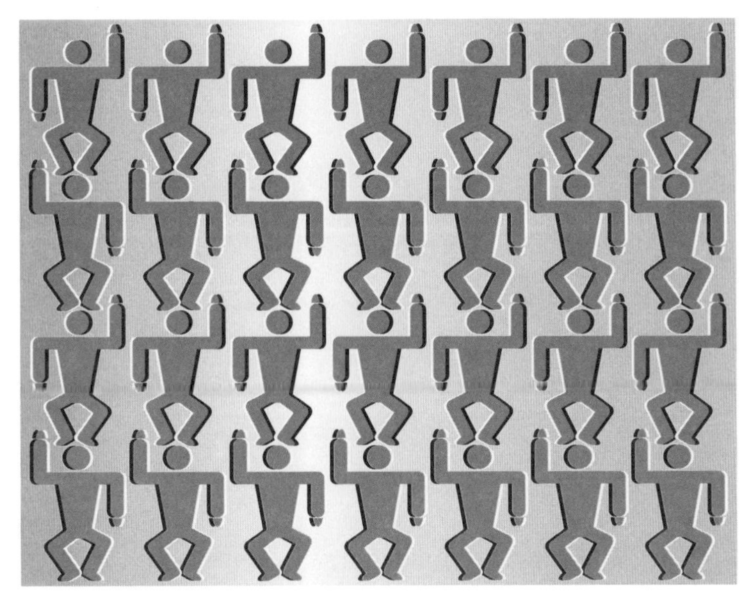

These silhouetted dancers appear to be swaying back and forth to an inaudible beat...

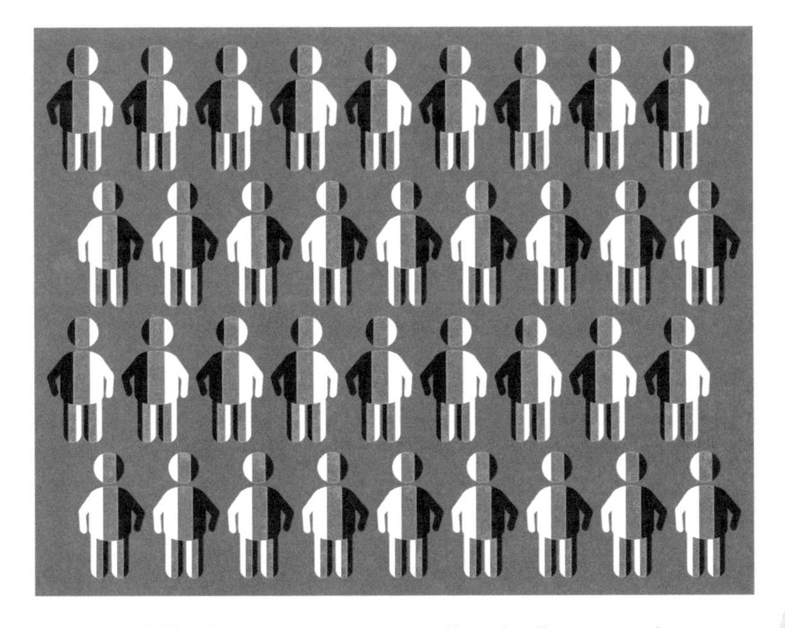

...while these people standing in line are also shifting back and forth to the same silent music.

FLIES IN SPACE

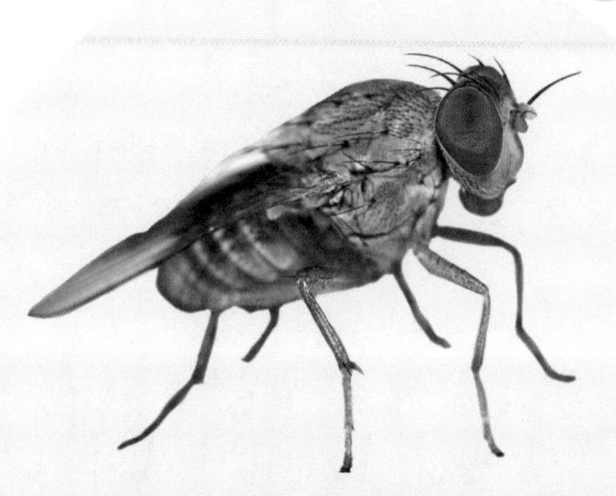

The first animals in space were fruit flies, sent up on a USA V-2 rocket in 1947 to test the effects of radiation exposure at high altitude. The fruit flies were later recovered alive.

NAMES OF THE WORLD

The most common first name in the world is Mohammed, while the most common surname is Chang.

DOTTY APPARITIONS

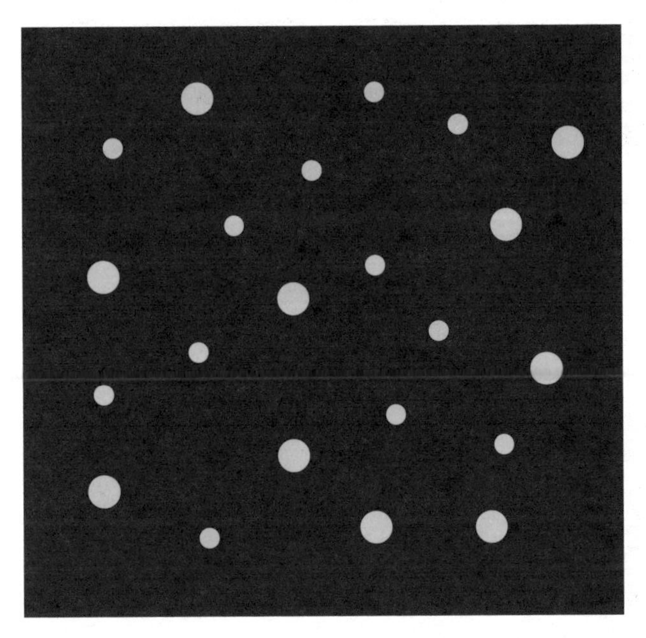

Stare at this image for a few seconds, then when you move your eyes from dot to dot you should see glowing orange-edged dots.

SLIDING VERTICALS

These red and blue tiles appear to be sliding up and down their columns. This effect appears because your brain is desperately trying to line them all up neatly!

SAME SIZE?

The upper red sphere looks bigger than the lower one, although in reality they are both printed at exactly the same size. The eye is correcting for the apparent distance variation shown by the chequerboard.

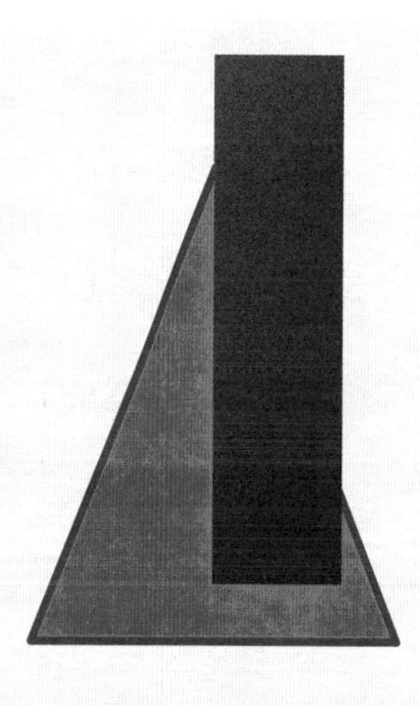

PERFECT TRIANGLE?

It looks like the right-hand side of this orange shape is at far too low an angle to form a perfect triangle with the rest of the visible shape, but this is just an illusion. You can use a ruler to prove that it meets up with the top of the triangle.

SLOGAN CLAIM

Many interpretations have been given to the meaning of the '57 varieties' claim on Heinz® bottles. The truth is that Henry Heinz, the company founder, chose '57' solely because '5' and '7' were his lucky numbers.

OLYMPIC ARTS

The modern Olympic Games once included art competitions, from 1912 until 1948. Medals were awarded for sports-themed artworks in five categories: painting, music, architecture, literature and sculpture. These competitions were called the 'Pentathlon of the Muses'.

SUPER HAIL

The largest hailstone ever officially recorded was a staggering 20 cm (8 in) wide and fell on the unlucky inhabitants of South Dakota, USA, in 2010. The heaviest recorded hailstone weighed a whopping 1 kg (2.25 lb) and fell in Bangladesh in 1986.

NOW YOU SEE IT...

This pseudo-3D optical illusion was created for an arts show in the Netherlands.

ROTATIONS IN BLUE

This seems to be a rather boring image, until you start to move the book slowly towards you. As the image moves closer, the blue shapes start to rotate around each wheel.

LET IT SNOW

Deadly asbestos fibre was used as fake snow in early Hollywood films, including *The Wizard of Oz* and *Holiday Inn*. Asbestos became expensive after World War Two, however, so was replaced with painted cornflakes. Falling cornflakes turned out to be too noisy, so for 1946's *It's a Wonderful Life* a new foam-based snow effect was developed – which has remained in use ever since.

ALIEN LIGHTS

In the original *Alien* movie, the alien egg chamber is lit via laser lighting that was actually for a nearby rehearsal by the rock band *The Who*!

IRREGULAR BALLS?

The circles in the image below seem to be vertically misaligned, but if you use a ruler you'll discover that they're actually all arranged in a perfectly straight line!

FADE OUT

Focus intently on the centre of this grey smudge, and you should find that after just a few seconds it starts to fade away. Keep looking at it and it will vanish completely!

NAME SEARCH

1

Search behemoth Google® is so-called thanks to the poor spelling of one of its founders. They intended it to be called Googol, after the very large number – one followed by a hundred zeroes – but accidentally registered the wrong domain and so decided to stick with the name. Meanwhile they call their headquarters the Googleplex, which is a reference to the related word 'googolplex' – ten to the power of a googol, a number so large that there isn't enough space in the entire universe to write it out in full!

POISONED CHALICE

The original actor playing the Tin Man in *The Wizard of Oz* was hospitalized because he was poisoned by the aluminium powder used in his make-up. He had to be replaced and did not then appear on-screen in the finished film. The replacement actor was given a safer paste-based make-up instead.

TALLER FIRST THING

You are typically 1–2.5 cm (0.4–1 in) taller when you get out of bed than you are by the end of the day. The bones in your spine are compressed by gravity and other activities throughout the day, shortening you. Astronauts in space can therefore be as much as 7.5 cm (3 in) taller than on Earth, due to the lack of gravity!

NUMBERING OF PARTS

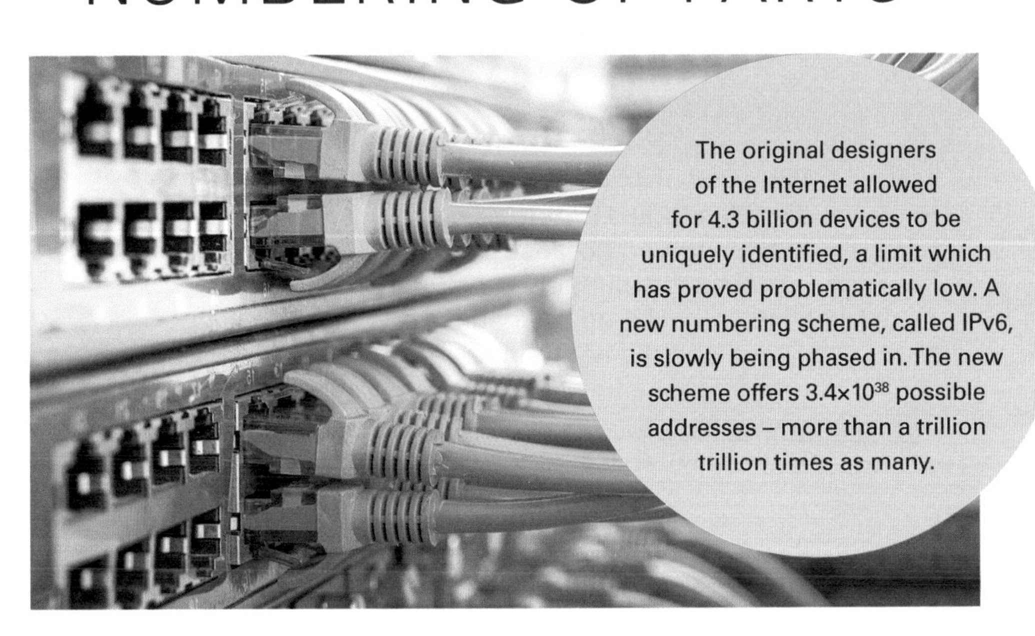

The original designers of the Internet allowed for 4.3 billion devices to be uniquely identified, a limit which has proved problematically low. A new numbering scheme, called IPv6, is slowly being phased in. The new scheme offers 3.4×10^{38} possible addresses – more than a trillion trillion times as many.

PAY THE TOLL

The highest toll ever paid to pass through the Panama Canal is 375,600 US dollars, although the average is around 54,000 US dollars. The lowest toll ever paid was in 1928, when swimmer Richard Halliburton paid 36 US cents to swim the canal.

MINCE MATTERS

The fruit-based mincemeat filling used in mince pies has no meat in it, but this has not always been the case. Until as recently as 100 years ago, a range of minced meats were frequently included in mince pies.

FIND THE SQUARE

This circle of dots hides a hidden square. Can you work out how to draw a perfect square that passes through every dot? The secret is to first group the dots into four pairs. Solution overleaf.

SAME SIZE?

Which of the horizontal rectangles do you think is exactly the same size as the vertical one? Amazingly, it's actually the central, orange one!

IN OTHER WORDS

A small number of words have multiple meanings in such a way that they can also be their own opposites! These are sometimes called 'contronyms'.

Examples include:

'dust'
– to add dust, or to remove dust

'overlook'
– to pay attention to, or to ignore

'cleave'
– to separate, or to join

'sanction'
– to give approval for something, or to penalize for doing something

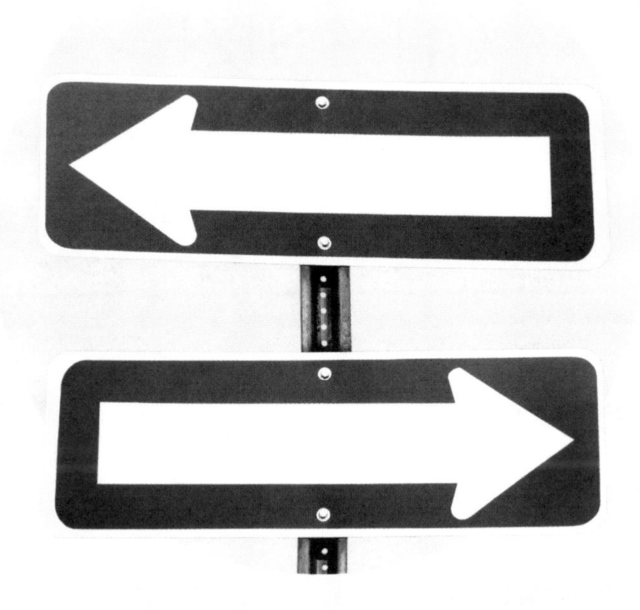

WORLD NUMBERS

In AD 1000 the world population was around 400 million. It took 750 years for the population to double to 800 million. Conversely, in 1960 there were 3 billion people on Earth and yet it took just 40 years for the population to double to 6 billion. The primary reason for this massive speed-up is a huge decline in early deaths.

CITY SIZE

Valencia is the name of the third-largest city in both Venezuela and Spain! Each city also has roughly 1.8 million inhabitants in their metropolitan areas.

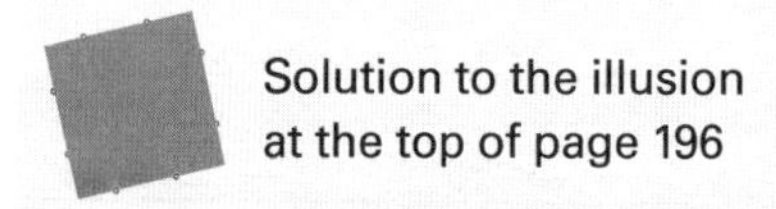

Solution to the illusion at the top of page 196

FUTURE PROOF

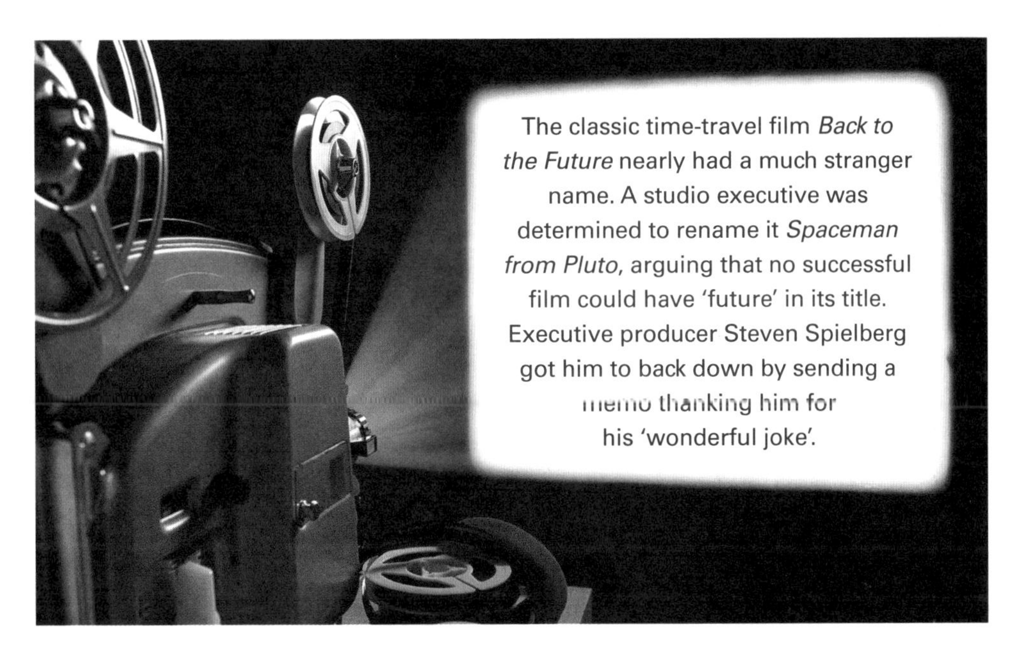

The classic time-travel film *Back to the Future* nearly had a much stranger name. A studio executive was determined to rename it *Spaceman from Pluto*, arguing that no successful film could have 'future' in its title. Executive producer Steven Spielberg got him to back down by sending a memo thanking him for his 'wonderful joke'.

PERFECT MATCH

The 1980s voice actors for Mickey Mouse and Minnie Mouse actually got married in real life! Meanwhile, Walt Disney claimed in a 1933 interview that Mickey and Minnie were married 'in private life'.

FLICKERING SQUARES

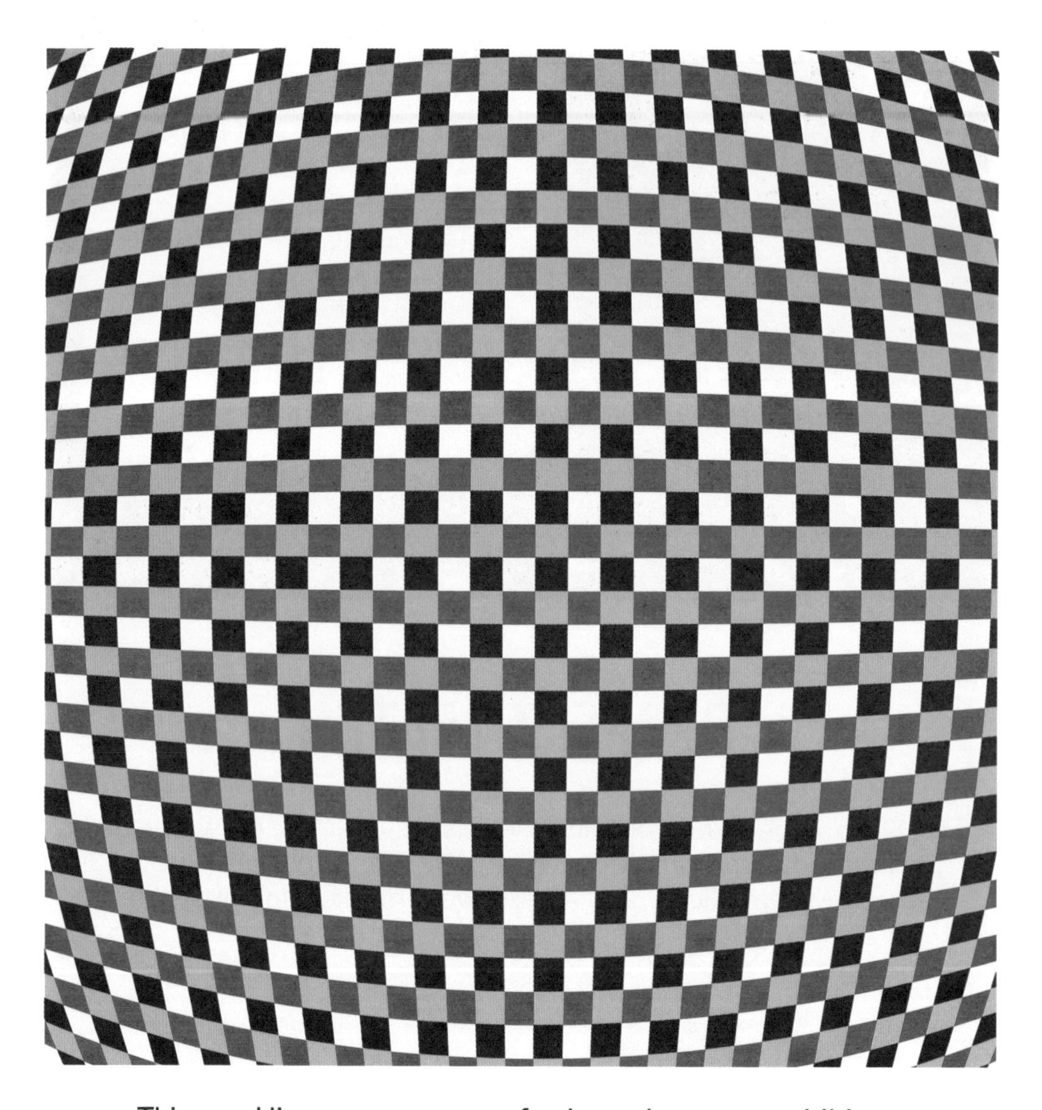

This sparkling arrangement of coloured squares exhibits a curious effect where the magenta squares seem to flicker and change colour as you move your eyes around the pattern.

GREEN BEACH

Hawaii's Papakolea beach has an extremely rare characteristic – the sand is green, due to crystals of olivine found in local rocks. The only other green beaches in the world are in Guam and in the Galapagos Islands.

@ SYMBOL

The @ symbol on the computer keyboard has a range of names in different countries, many based on its appearance. The Italians call it a snail, while the Dutch call it a monkey tail.

SUPER SALES

Jeans were invented in 1871 and patented by Levi Strauss in 1873. In the USA alone, over 15 billion US dollars-worth of jeans are sold each year.

PET NAMES

Charles Dickens used to refer to his wife in letters as 'dearest darling Pig', or 'dearest Mouse'. It is presumed that this was meant affectionately!

KEEP DANCING

Natalie Portman dislocated a rib during filming of *Black Swan*, in which she played a prima ballerina – and then discovered that the film's budget was so low that there was no medic. She gave up her trailer so that a medic could be hired.

SHIMMER AND SHAKE

There appears to be a flower-like shape in the centre of this vibrating, flickering pattern, created through the interference of the narrow lines. This is called a Moiré pattern.

IN LARGE NUMBERS

2			4		3			8
				6				
		4	9		8	6		
7		3				4		6
	9			7			5	
6		1				8		7
		8	7		6	1		
				4				
5			3		2			4

There are 6,670,903,752,021,072,936,960 (6.67×10^{21}) possible different ways to fill an empty Sudoku grid. Each of these solutions in turn has an extremely large number of possible puzzles that result in that solution. It's therefore extraordinarily unlikely that you will encounter the same puzzle twice, just by chance!

NO WIN

The record for the most Oscar® nominations without a win is held by sound re-recording mixer Kevin O'Connell, who has been nominated 20 times without success. Prior to this, film composer Victor Young was also nominated 20 times without winning, but then did succeed on the 21st attempt. Unfortunately he died prior to the awards ceremony, and the Oscar® was given posthumously.

HIGH JUMP

The highest ever jump from the top of a building was from the top of the 828 m (2,717 ft) Burj Khalifa in Dubai, United Arab Emirates. French BASE jumpers Fred Fugen and Vince Reffet leapt from a platform specially built on top of the building.

PATTERN RIPPLES

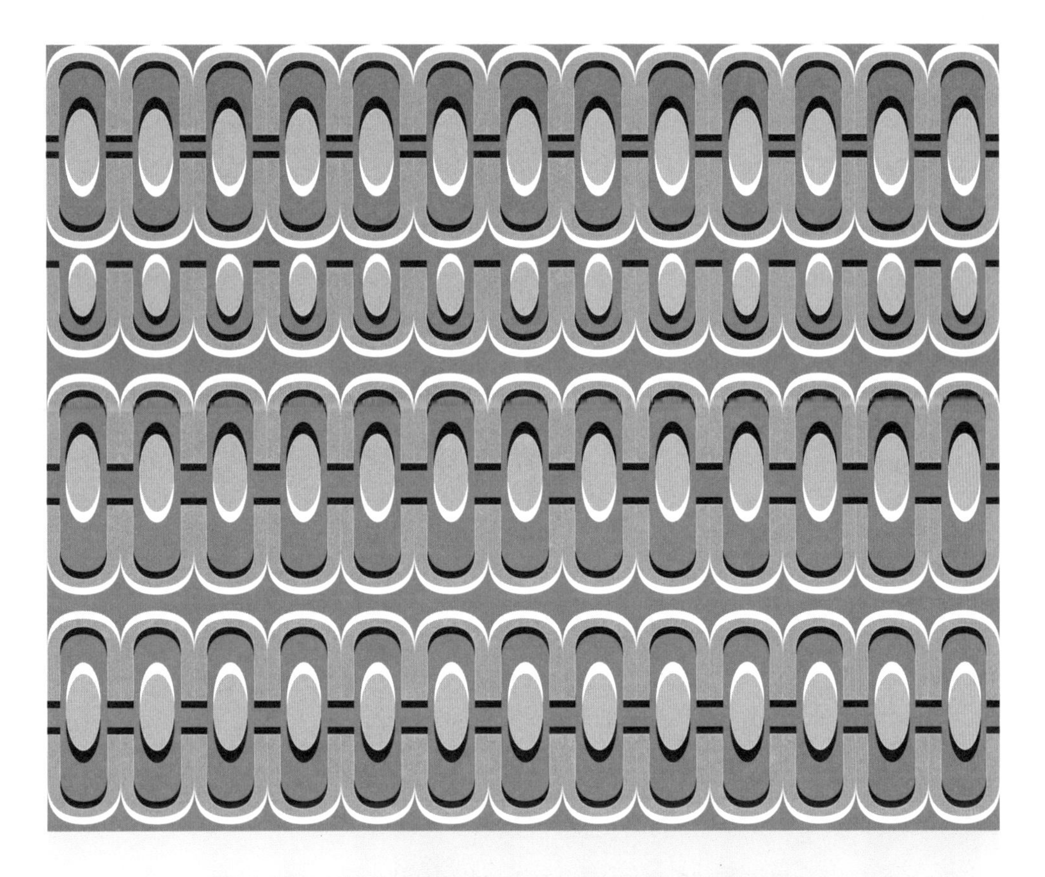

This South American-esque pattern appears
to ripple up and down as you cast your eyes over it.

WHICH WAY?

Do you see a large number of black arrows facing down, or a lot of yellow arrows facing up?

ON ALL SIDES

This looks like a wire-framed cube, but if you try tracing around the edges you'll soon discover that you'd have a problem if you tried adding a solid face to each side!

ANIMAL THREATS

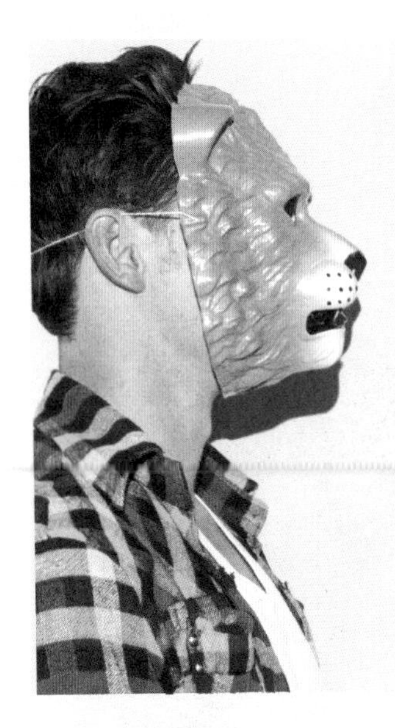

In early Puritan America, people who looked like animals were sometimes put to death on the charge of being the offspring of animals themselves!

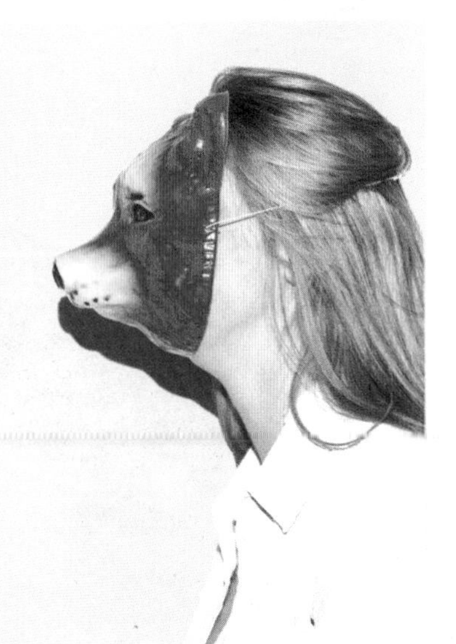

PLACE OF HORROR

The classic horror film *The Shining* was filmed on the site of what is now Albert Square, part of the set of long-running British soap *EastEnders*, at Elstree Studios in north-west London.

FIRST ON FILM

Back to the Future 2 features the first film appearance of Elijah Wood, who went on to play the lead character in the *Lord of the Rings* trilogy. He is one of the two boys playing video games who speaks to Marty near the start of the film.

HOLES AND HEXAGONS

This grid of circular holes looks oddly hexagonal if you view it from a distance – give it a try!

DON'T BE SQUARE

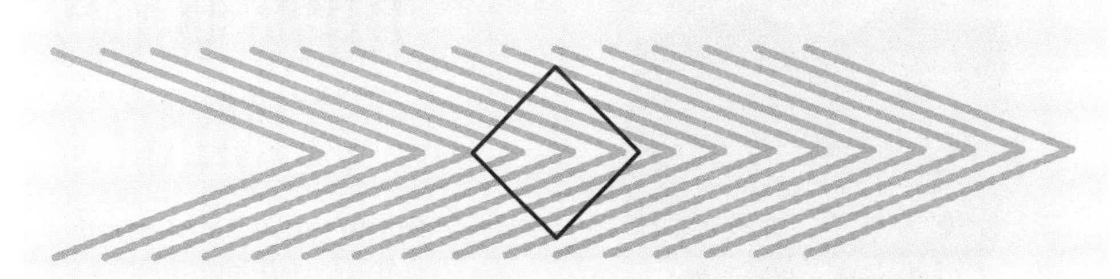

In this variant of the Orbison illusion (see page 74), this perfect square appears distorted – the right-hand side looks shorter than the left-hand side.

CREEPY CRAWLY

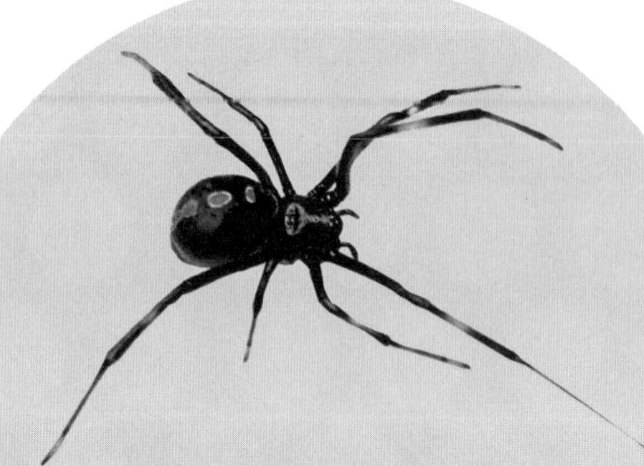

In the 2002 *Spider-Man* film, when Peter Parker is bitten by a black widow spider, the producers actually painted a less dangerous spider, *Steatoda grossa*, the 'false black widow', with blue and red stripes.

HOW MANY TIMES?

In the film *Love Actually*, the word 'actually' is spoken by the characters a total of 22 times.

EVERLASTING WATER

This peaceful-looking structure includes a water feature that any gardener would be proud of – a waterfall that never runs out of water and doesn't even require a pump to keep it flowing!

SPIN ME ROUND

This pattern consists of concentric circles of differently coloured lighter beads which, combined with darker beads between them, results in the illusion of a slowly rotating image. The colours in this pattern make it very hard to look at, encouraging you to look away!

TONGUE-TASTIC

The human tongue can detect five primary tastes: bitter, sour, salty, sweet and umami. Umami is best described as a savoury or meaty taste. The tongue itself contains a few thousand taste buds, each in turn holding around a hundred taste receptor cells. These receptor cells are lost with age, however, as taste perception fades – by adulthood around half are gone.

SPARE TYRES

The LEGO® group is one of the world's most prolific tyre manufacturers, producing over 650 million tiny tyres each year.

TOUGH EGG

If you hold the top and bottom of an egg between your finger tips, you won't be able to break the egg just by squeezing your fingers together. This is because the pressure is distributed evenly across the egg, unlike when you crack its side.

NUMBER CRUNCHING

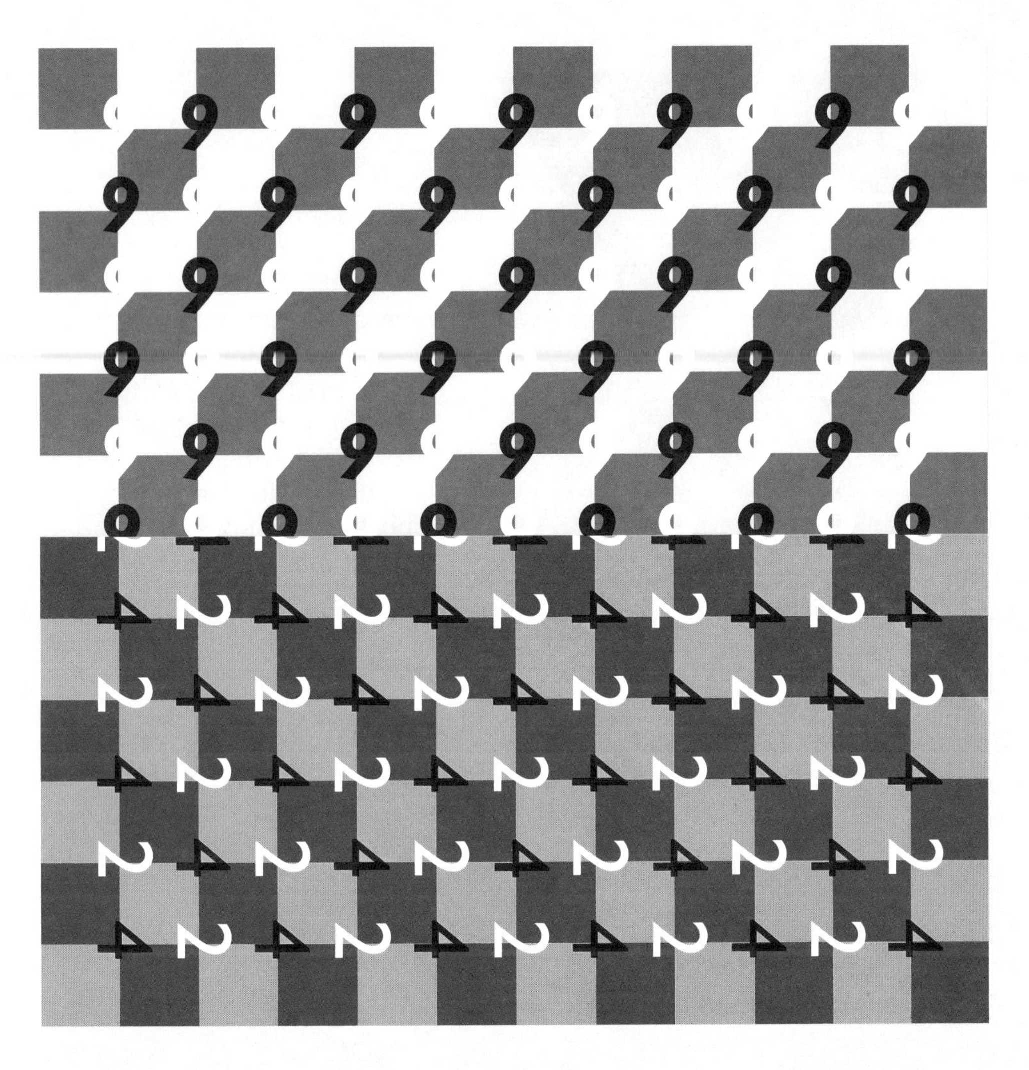

These chequered patterns don't appear to be quite true thanks to the overlaid numbers. The top image appears to lean a little, while the bottom image appears to lean at an even greater angle.

SHADY SHAPES

It's said that 'X marks the spot' – but in this case the X itself has more than the average amount of mystery about it! Consider for example the line of the 'X' from top-right to bottom-centre – it appears aligned, but it's clear from the bottom-right of the shape that this is impossible!

This shape would be as impossible to make as the 'X' in the image above. If you're not convinced then just give it a go!

BIG MOUTH

During pre-production of *Jaws*, George Lucas got his head stuck in a model shark mouth, after Steven Spielberg closed it for a joke and then discovered that the controls were malfunctioning and he was unable to open it again!

A FUTURE FOR MUM

The Disney® film studio turned down the chance to make *Back to the Future* because they thought the mother-and-son relationship in the film was too risqué.

SINGLE OUT

In Bolivia, you have to be aged 18 to vote if you are married, but if you are single then you must wait 3 more years until you are 21! Voting is also a legal requirement.

FAST TRACK

The fastest animal on the planet is the cheetah, which is able to reach speeds of up to 75 mph (120 km/h).

UNDER THE SUN

The Sun is 149.6 million km (93 million miles) from the Earth. That's 180,000 times the height of the world's tallest building, the Burj Khalifa.

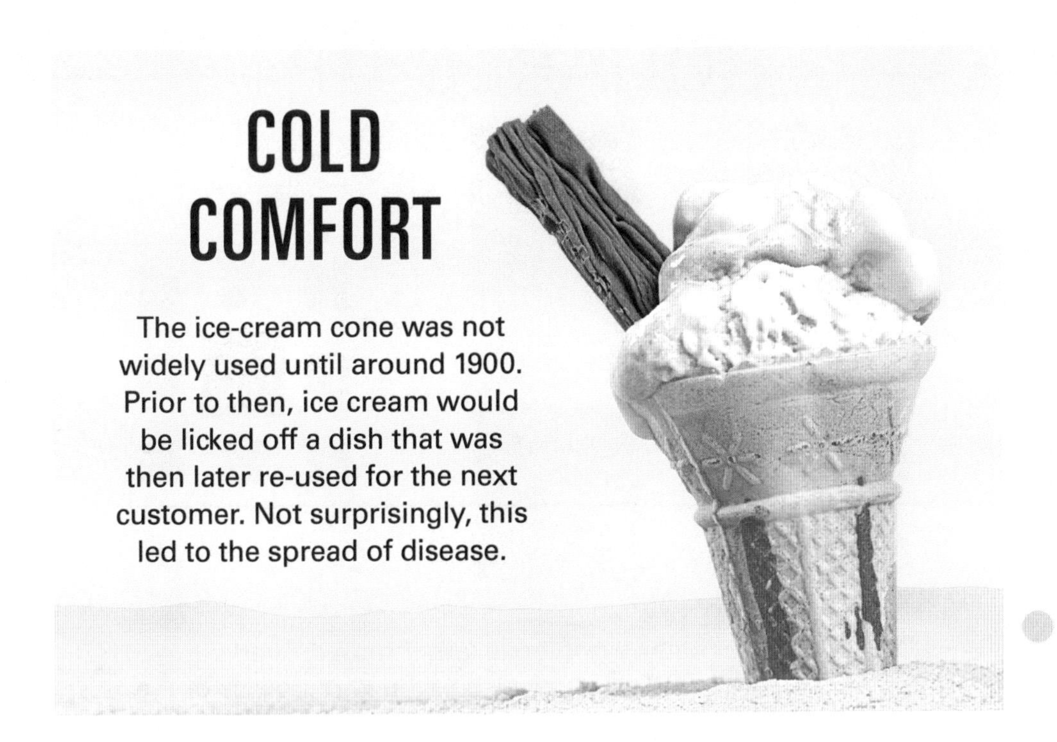

COLD COMFORT

The ice-cream cone was not widely used until around 1900. Prior to then, ice cream would be licked off a dish that was then later re-used for the next customer. Not surprisingly, this led to the spread of disease.

CAT TRAP

Is the cat sitting on a step, or is it hovering between stairs? The answer depends on whether you look at the top half or the bottom half of this drawing!

SQUARED UP

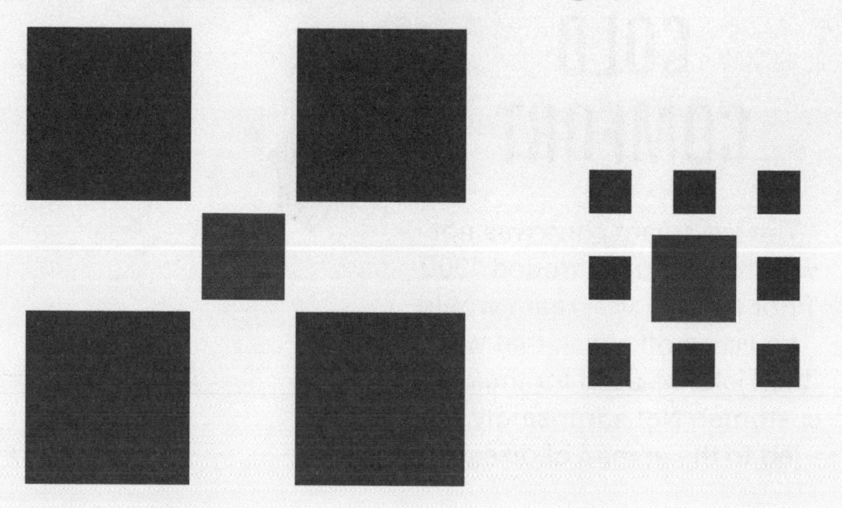

The red square on the right looks larger than the red square on the left, but this is only because of the varying size of the surrounding squares. In reality, both red squares are identical.

JUMP THE Q

In all standard English words, a letter 'q' must be followed by a 'u'. The only exceptions in standard dictionaries come from terms imported from other languages, such as 'qintar', an Albanian monetary unit, and 'niqab', a veil that some Muslim women wear.

BIG FRUIT

The largest fruit ever grown was a pumpkin that weighed more than a tonne, weighing in at 1,056 kg (2,328 lb).

KALEIDOSCOPE

This illusion combines a rotating centre and an expanding outer portion for a visual double-whammy!